HOW TO SURVIVE ANYTHING

The life story of David & Yetta Kane

Editor: Elaine Ash
Transcriber: Andrea Fox
Book Design: Joanne Bolton
Graphic Design: Alex Kane and Lindsay Lassen

ISBN: 978-1-4507-9133-5. This Edition is limited to 2,000 copies.

For press inquiries, reprints or excerpts please contact
Elaine Ash @ ashedit@gmail.com

Printed in China through Bolton Associates,
San Rafael, CA   www.boltonprinting.com

Photographs: *Page 1:* A painting depicting the Tree of Life by Barbara Pereira Bastos (Hebrew name, Brachayafa), one of the Rabbi's conversion/reversion students. Beshert means "meant to be."
Opposite Title page: Yetta and Rabbi Kane on their 45th anniversary cruise.
Copyright page: The wedding party, details on page 57.

DEDICATION

Dedicated to the blessed memory of our parents,

grandparents and our extended Jewish family—

the six million souls and one-and-a-half million children

who perished in the Nazi holocaust.

$\mathcal{I}$NTRODUCTION

$\mathcal{W}$e wrote this book because many, many people throughout the years have asked us to write a book about our experiences. For 59 years now, we have been married and lived an exemplary life, and we say this with all gratitude to God. This memoir is a gift to our children, grandchildren and great-grandchildren, that they should have an idea of who we are, what we are, and what we stood for.

When we were young, entering our new life in America, we were trying so hard, going to school, working in the army, and building a family. We had already survived the holocaust and escaped abuse, indignities, and the horrors of war. So we embraced our wonderful new country, America, and we pushed the past to the backs of our minds. Yet we never forgot it.

People ask, "Where is God?" God is where you invite him. God was

1950: David and Yetta on Santa Monica Beach.
Young, in love, and having fun.

invited in when we first met as a couple, and into our home when we got married.

God is our guide. Now that the years have gone on, we can see many lessons learned from the past, good and bad. We learned from what we so painfully went through, and also what we joyfully went through. What we learned, we applied to creating a happy, successful life. We were the American dream come true, and we still are, even today.

God blessed us with good children, good people who love God and respect others and work hard, so we decided to leave this book as a special gift for them, and generations to come. We hope this book can make a difference in their lives and perhaps, in the lives of everyone who reads it.

David and Yetta Kane

Long Beach, California

October, 2011

God is where you invite him.

TABLE OF CONTENTS

Yetta's original family home in Myadel, Poland. This is the house shared by Edla, Zelik and their children, also grandparents Yakov Shlomo and Sorehfreide, in happier days before the war.

Picture taken by Mr. Mones Zelik in 2003.

Chapter One

A few words here and now

Before we start to talk about the past, let's talk a little about the present. Here and now in 2011, we are happy and healthy for the most part, thank God, and we just welcomed our first great-grandchild into the world. This in itself is the greatest miracle and blessing anyone can have happen in their life. So we are extraordinarily lucky. We have a beautiful home on a park, right down the street from our daughter, Bryna, and our son-in-law, Jerry Kaufman, and our dear grandchildren. We have enjoyed rich, full lives personally and professionally, and continue to enjoy a fulfilling, meaningful retirement. Our work is never done, and our lives are abundantly blessed.

As everyone who lives to their senior years knows, life has its ups and downs. As soon as we came to America, life started going well for us. But it was not always so. Our lives, like so many other Jews born before World War II, took drastic turns. Some people did not survive. We did. And for that we are supremely grateful. Let's start at the beginning...

YETTA'S GIRLHOOD

My maiden name was Istrin, Yetta Istrin. I was born in Myadel, Poland. One time it was Prussia, one time it was Lithuania and the country kept going back and forth, until it was occupied by Germany. In the little *shtetl* where we lived, which is a Yiddish word for *a small village*, we had a shul and we lived with neighbors on very, very good terms and we had a beautiful life. I would say we were middle class, and I was born on December 28, 1932.

Myadel Poland. Left to right: Edla, Tante Kala, Motle, Zeyde Berle, Moshe Josky. Front: Baske

My mother's name was Edla and my father was Zelik. My father was very strong, very religious, but modern. My parents believed in God, mankind, and they believed there would be a better tomorrow. I had two brothers and a sister; Morris, Herman and Mini, the baby. My dear sister Sara had not been born yet.

We had horses, cows and chickens. Everything we had came from our garden and everything was made by hand. We did not have stores where you could go out and buy groceries. The butter had to be made, the cheese had to be made, the milk had to be milked from the cow, the fish had to be caught and so on. We leased two or three hectares of land from a rich person, a *poretz*, like a landlord or land baron, leasing out land to people who wished to farm it, cultivate it and harvest it.

We leased the land, and my parents hired people to plant, harvest, and bring in straw and hay for the winter, for the animals. We had big barns, three or four cows and a whole flock of chickens.

My grandparents, my father's parents, lived with us. My grandmother's first name was Sorehfreide, and my grandfather was Yakov Shlomo. Sorehfreide was only 55 or 60 years old back then. She was very pretty with sparkling blue eyes and her hair pulled back in a chignon. The only time I saw her with her hair down was in the *mikvah*, the ritual bath. Every day, she wore a clean apron, made with her own hands. She sewed clothes for the non-Jewish people and made money for our family that way. My grandfather Yakov was a farmer and worked in the fields with my father.

We had a house like a duplex where they lived in one part and we lived in the other. But for whatever reason, I don't remember, the windows were boarded up because the war was coming. They used to bake their own bread and make everything. Sorehfreide sewed for us and for other people. Both Edla, my mother, and my grandmother would tend to the house and we children milked the cows, doing everything that was necessary.

In Europe, when you had people working for you, they went out to the field about 6:00 or 7:00 A.M. to plow or to get the potatoes or cut the hay or straw, or harvest the grain. They had to be fed. My family fed them breakfast and took lunch to the field to feed them. If you had three or four men working, you had to have a lot of food. And the basic breakfast would be, for the summer, potatoes of course, homemade bread, homemade cheese, plenty of butter and beet borscht, or it could also be made with cucumbers. You'd have the cold borscht with cucumbers and lots of sour cream in it. And that was their breakfast. For lunch, you would take them cold tea when it was hot and again you would take the bread and cheese and sandwiches.

We also had a small store for dry goods. My father went to Vilna once a week after the Sabbath, after the *Havdala*. He would drive the whole night with a horse and buggy. He would arrive in Vilna about 6:00 or 7:00 A.M. in the morning. He took a gun with him, which was not that common. It wasn't like now where you have money in the bank and write a check. Then, you paid in cash. If you were a client for a long time, maybe, they might give you credit. But my father always took the money to pay for everything.

He bought goods for our family and also to sell to others in the village; oil, kerosene, sugar, salt, pepper, cocoa, chicory and sewing things. Sometimes, he'd bring halva or candy, but basically he bought the things we didn't grow in our garden or on the farm. And then he bought more goods and sold it to the people that did not go to the big city, which was some hours away. My father would also take orders—everything for sewing and making clothes. He collected payment in advance for the orders, and took a commission for his services, and that's how he made a living. We always had nice clothes and a nice house until the war started.

Our house had a big oven, like a pizza oven that was our means to bake food and keep the house warm. You could bake about twenty pounds of bread at a time. The oven kept the house warm, and when it was very cold, a person could sleep on top of it.

When I woke up at dawn, or earlier, the cows were milked already. I could smell the fresh bread baking. On Thursday, Sorehfreide and Edla would start baking for Saturday—rolls, twists, cinnamon rolls and tortes. We made lots of jam and preserves: loganberry, gooseberry, raspberry and cherry. We had no refrigeration, just a cold cellar to keep things fresh and cool. We even made our own cheese.

On the farm, we entertained ourselves. It wasn't like today where a child has toys and more toys. We would get a book sometimes, or Sorehfreide would take little scraps of material, stuff it with dirt, sew it up and then draw little eyes and a nose and a smile and make me a doll. To feed my doll I would pretend to make little pancakes.

I was sent to collect eggs from the chicken coop. We had a long stick like a hoe—a stick with a piece of metal on the end, and we would

Left to right: Zelik, Yetta, Edla, Herman, Morris. Front: Baby Sara. 1949

pull out the eggs. I would also take a few eggs to play at cooking. I would make a little hole in the mud, it wasn't sand, it was mud, and make a few little mud pancakes and dry them. And that's how we entertained ourselves. My parents bought me a guitar—a beautiful, blonde guitar. I was going to start lessons, but the war ended that and I never bought another guitar or took a lesson.

I also remember we had a horse and cart for transportation, and I could ride the horse anytime I wanted, when I was not in the field, or the horse was not working. The horse's name was Sierkah (Seer-kah). I could get on him bareback—no saddle, just a bridle. He would put out his foot and I would hang onto his mane and climb up and ride. If he went down a steep hill, I would slide right over his head! And Sierkah would stop, put out his foot, and I'd climb back up. So that was my entertainment, and my girlhood in a little *shtetl* in Poland.

DAVID'S BOYHOOD

I was born Dawid Josef Koplowicz, July 29th, 1928, in the city of Bedin, Poland. It was a fair-sized city; there were at one time, 60,000 residents, of which half were Jewish—or more than half. I was born, I believe, in a hospital in Krakow—it wasn't at home. My mother, Brajndla, blessed memory, was a certified mid-wife, almost like a Ph.D. in gynecology. She worked with many gynecologists and delivered two thousand children before the war. I was born to two wonderful parents. My father, Kople (Karol) was an administrator of buildings before the war and also worked in hardware stores.

When I was born, they had to use forceps to get my head out. My mother was in labor for something like 36 hours. They brought me home to our beautiful apartment—nicely set up, and we lived on one of the main streets in our town. In the whole town, there were three telephones and we had one of them. The police station, the city hall/fire station and my mother. She had to have it for her profession.

We had help. I had nannies—Polish-Jewish nannies, and I had beautiful grandparents. I would often visit them and my grandmother, Reizel, used to carry me around in her hands. She was a little lady—maybe an inch shorter than my wife. Reizel had a big shawl that she would wrap around to carry me everywhere—even to the bakery to buy me some sweets. She always made things for me—whatever I wanted to eat. She was very religious, a great mother and a wonderful wife. She was a blonde—a rarity in Polish Jewry. She had a smile as big as the state of California, and never had an unkind word. She was a happy woman. She spoiled my father and made him feel like a king. Even as a little boy, I took notice of that and the love that was showered on me. I also felt I was somebody special.

My grandfather, Menachem Mendel, was the only one that had a beard. My father didn't have a beard. Menachem worked in a meat processing plant and he had a tiny aluminum box with candies in it. He always had a candy for me. Every week we did a different parsha from the Torah, and he would recite.

If there ever was an example of a love affair between husband and wife, that was it. Menachem never had a cross word for Reizel. My grandparents took care of me a lot because my parents both had jobs and were busy working. I had a little sister named Pearl (pronounced Pear-ill), and we also called her Polesia, which is a term of endearment for a little girl. I had three aunts and later on, some cousins. It was a nice-sized family.

At the age of five, I started going to a Hebrew day school and at the age of six I started going to religious school, as well, in the afternoon.

Love at first sight:
DAVID MEETS YETTA

David

We met officially in Los Angeles, California in June of 1950. I was doing a little singing at the Park Manor. Becky Burke, the woman who owned the place, asked me to sing. Becky was a sweet, little Jewish mother, and she always had some extra food for me. Yetta's girlfriend, Malah, asked me to go with her to a refugee dance there. We went with a very, very expensive transportation—a $50,000 bus. Malah introduced me to Yetta. She was sitting between her two brothers, Morris and Herman, one on either side like guards. Yetta was wearing a red sweater. I remember the red sweater exactly, and she had that smile on her face and I dared to ask her to dance. As we danced, I fell head over heels in love right then and there. I forgot the brothers and everything else, and kissed her on the forehead. The response to that was I got slapped across my face. I got a little peeved about that, but two weeks later, I couldn't take it anymore and I called her.

My father liked Malah. I told my father, "That's fine, but between Malah and me, there's no chemistry." I called to invite Yetta to my birth-

David courting Yetta during a day's leave from Fort Ord. Brother Herman chaperones from the car on Waring Avenue.

day. She accepted, but I didn't exactly tell her it was my birthday. She lived on the west side, the Fairfax area, and I lived in Boyle Heights. So she had to take the expensive transportation to come see me. I had invited five other fellows to my birthday and she was the only girl. And my father, Kople, blessed memory, was there and my stepmother, Helen, the lovely lady he married after the war. Yetta turned red as a beet when she got there, because she was the only girl.

Needless to say, we continued seeing each other. The more I saw her, the more I loved her. I set my feet on the fact that she was going to be my gal. By that time, from June to October, 1950, we were pretty much in love with each other.

I was already driving a '39 Oldsmobile, which my friend, Julius Solnit, sold to me for $150. Actually, he gave it to me like a present, because it was the dirtiest car I've ever driven—it was like a Bonnie and Clyde type of car. I was driving it because I had to go for my induction into the army. If I hadn't been drafted, I would never have become a citizen. So I was willing to do whatever was necessary. Also, Yetta, God bless her, who is a very deep-thinking and feisty type of woman, said to me, "Listen, if we're going to be a couple, you're going to go into the army." So that was that.

Kople tried to talk me into going to Mexico so I could avoid being sent to the war in Korea. He said he would send me packages there. But instead,

Kople and David in the Displaced Persons Camp, Landsberg am Lech, Germany. David got a special permit for the American rifle. 1945–46

I became a chaplain's assistant at Fort Ord, California. I stayed there for two years, and in the meantime Yetta and I corresponded.

I was coming back and forth to Los Angeles by expensive transportation and sometimes getting rides with other people at Fort Ord who had cars. I paid a few dollars to share the ride for the weekend. I would get a pass to travel, and I came to Los Angeles to see my darling. I had proposed to her maybe 10, 15 times, and she always said, "No, let's wait, because my brothers and parents feel I should wait." After all, she was just sixteen-and-a-half when we met, and they thought, rightfully so, that she hadn't seen the world, and this and that and the other thing, and here she's going to get tied up with this guy... Suffice it to say, that she had a reason to want to wait awhile, because in the Army, you never knew where you were going. I could have been sent to Korea. I wasn't, but we didn't know that.

After 15 proposals, I told her, "Next time you want to get married, you ask me." And so it was. She wrote me a letter and a friend of mine who was another chaplain's assistant, Paul McCurty, read between the lines and said, "Hey stupid, she wants to get married." So I called and sure enough we were married on January 19, 1952. The 19th is a very favorite date on our calendar, because I came here on May 19th, she came November 19th, and we got married January 19th. I feel my life began when I met my wife.

My friend, Julius Solnit, who became like a second father to me said, "David, if I were your age you wouldn't have a chance in hell to get Yetta. You better stick around and don't you let loose of her."

Woman praying in front of Shabbat candles. One of
Yetta's favorite images that hangs in David's study.

Yetta in Hasencheke, Germany. Displaced Persons
Camp. 1947–1948

Chapter Two

In Chapter One, we reminisced about our childhoods in Europe, with our beloved parents. Then we skipped a few years to talk about the happy times when we met and courted as a young couple, during our first years in America. And we planned this book that way, so that readers would know that we survived and happy times came to us. But now it's time to talk about weightier things—years that shaped us during World War II and events that solidified our faith as Jews, even as it tore our families and homes apart. Our story goes back again to 1939…

YETTA REMEMBERS WARTIME

The Germans were in town already, and my little sister, my sweetheart Mini, was sick. She had golden blonde curls and blue eyes. Mini was just two years old, and she caught measles or chicken pox. She had spots on her little face, that's all I knew. There were doctors around, but we had no medicine, and Mini died of fever in my arms. Maybe if she had lived, we wouldn't be alive, because with a baby you couldn't run that far. Babies need food and attention, and to be dry and warm, and we never had that, as soon as we started running.

Yetta's original family home in Myadel, Poland.

I was not quite eight years old when the Germans came. We were with the Germans for six or seven months before the SS came in. The people who came first were in the war in 1914, when Prussia and Germany were fighting. Basically, they didn't touch anybody, only the people they were fighting, the men. So we stayed. But when the Germans did come in, the Wermacht, the ones that came in to prepare the city for the Gestapo, they talked to my parents. Edla and Zelik understood German, many languages. And in German they said to my parents, "You poor Jews, you should run. We don't want to do you any harm. However, when the SS comes, you are going to be in trouble."

Zelik was around 36 or 37 years old and he said, "Where can we go?" He knew that if we went by horse and buggy, and thieves saw that there was a family, and figured we had money and belongings, they would kill us.

We lived in a corner house on a big street and when the tanks and the Germans started coming in, our house was literally shaking like an earthquake from the heavy tanks and equipment and the motorcycles, and those Volkswagens—the big ones. When I see them now, or helmets like the Germans wore, up to this day, it gives me the heebie-jeebies. Our house is still standing, by the way. I have a picture. Some people live in it.

Around that time. my grandfather Yakov Shlomo developed psoriasis all over his body with painful, open sores. Edla took care of him lovingly and carefully until he died, and we buried him in the Jewish cemetery.

We stayed and then one day all the Jewish people had to go to work for the Germans. If you didn't, they kept killing people. My first introduction to the Germans was on a Saturday afternoon after Temple. At the time I was a towhead, blonde, blonde, and I was playing with the neighbor's little girl outside. At the same time, a Jewish man, tall and handsome, walked by. A German Gestapo was also going by in a uniform, dressed with pistols. The girl said, "Jude," which means *Jew.* Without saying one word, the Gestapo pulled out his gun and shot the man. He died right in front of us.

Every Sunday they used to make the Jewish men carry a big crucifix down to the lake and into the water. My older brother and father and other men all went. The Germans were in rowboats, following with guns until they could see that the men could no longer walk. Then they would start laughing and making fun and make them walk back. That was the Sunday routine.

My older brother Herman went, and one day they said they wanted to meet all the big shots of the city—the mayor, the judge, the doctors, the *shochet,* the *mohel,* all the rabbis, all the dignitaries of our small community.

There were about 25 or 30 men. Edla's brother, Motle, he was there and my mother had an older brother, a *procurer*, a prosecuting attorney. My two uncles and many other relatives were there too, and they said that all the men had to report because there was going to be a meeting.

Zelik said to Edla, "I don't like the 'smecht' (smell) of it, I don't like the feel of it. I'm not going. When they come back, they'll tell me what went on."

They took all those men in trucks out of the city and had them dig a grave. They killed all of them. Some of the people told us that the ground was shaking for days because they didn't want to waste bullets. Some of the people were not dead, they were just wounded, buried under the other bodies. That was the end of my relatives, and then my father was in hiding. Shortly after that, my Uncle Segaczyk (Segal-chick) and my family, they joined the Partisans. They were fighting the Germans, like gorilla fighting, blowing up trains, lifting the railroads so they couldn't go through, burning bridges—doing things to stop them from delivering munitions. We fought the Germans without any ammunition, with very, very little to fight with.

Uncle Segaczyk sent somebody for me. He had a little girl, who maybe at the time was two years old or so, and she was also a towhead. They were a few hours from where we lived, in a village where mostly non-Jewish people lived. He asked a man to go pick up his daughter, Clara, and me, and bring us to the village. That man put his life in jeopardy. If one of the neighbors had accused him of harboring Jewish children, his life would have ended too. He was taking a chance, but we spoke the same language, we wore the same clothes and we were blonde. We didn't look any different than the peasants. The only thing that divided us was religion. We were Jewish and they were Catholic. He put little babushkas, little scarves, on us and said if anybody stopped us, to say he took us to the other town to see a doctor because we were sick. And he brought us back to the village. But Clara's father said he was in danger of having his house burned down. So with that kind of warning, he couldn't refuse, and he told my parents to run away that night.

My grandmother Sorehfriede, decided that she would not run with us, she would stay in the house. She said to Edla and Zelik, "You children go. The neighbors love me, the Germans won't bother me, whatever will be, will be."

My whole family ran away and that was the last time I saw my home. After that, we were without a roof over our heads for a couple of years.

After we left, the Germans came and shot Sorehfreide. Our Jewish neighbors came and got her and buried her in the Jewish cemetery. She didn't suffer, and they didn't drag her anyplace. She was in her home when she was shot. My sister Sara, was named for her, later.

The other little girl, Clara, was left with a Christian family and her father told them, "If I survive the war, I will come and get her. If not, you can raise her as your own." She wasn't quite two years old. She stayed with that family, and her mother and father survived the war. After the war they came to pick her up. They came every day a little bit to be with her and get acquainted and to talk to her. But they were strangers to her. She had gone to church with her Christian family, and grew up like a little peasant girl with all the children. She would cry and finally after a month or so, they took her with them and within a year she died. She was taken away from

Passover Atarah, sterling, 6.5 kilos. Money and valuables were forbidden to be removed from Hungary after the war, but religious objects like this one were allowed.

the family she knew to be with strangers—a different way of life in a big city and so they lost her. They had two other children after the war.

We were on the run—we were in the woods and we were hiding. We were playing cat and mouse with the Germans. They were in one part, we were in the other. In order to survive, we had to cross bridges and rivers at night while they had the German Shepherds guarding every kilometer. They had a guard, guarding the railroad or important roads, so they could deliver food, deep into conquered Russia and other parts of the war.

WE WERE WITH THE PARTISANS, even though my father couldn't take part too much in the fighting, with three children beside him. But we followed the Partisans. We had to march sometimes eight hours without a stop in the pitch black of the night. We were running away from the fighting—deeper towards Russia. My father tied a towel, a rag, around my wrist and tied my older brother Morris to the other hand, and he dragged us. We would fall and he would pick us up. I weighed maybe 77 pounds. I was very, very thin. I was healthy and strong, but very thin, very petite and tiny. Herman and my mother always walked in front or behind. We were so hungry without sleep, cold. I never asked for food because I knew my parents didn't have it.

Sometimes, if we were near a field, my father would go steal potatoes or steal a chicken or something. Sometimes the Partisans would find a sheep or a lamb and slaughter it and we would have some food. Sometimes somebody from the village would tell the Germans that there were Partisans in the area and they would send soldiers with ammunition and trucks fully loaded, and they would kill everybody. So the Partisans started warning people in the villages that if they told the Germans we were there, their villages would be burned to the ground. After the Partisans burned a few villages, they didn't tell the Germans too often. They just didn't say anything—they didn't see anybody.

Some people were nice along the way and would let us into their bath houses. They were like saunas today, made of cedar and pine, with hot steam and water, not just a regular shower. They would let us sleep on the floor where it was warm and clean. Taking a bath was very, very seldom. They would stand guard in case somebody squealed to the Germans. Sometimes, while you were doing all that, there would come a person, a lookout or a guard, saying they think they heard something; that there might be Germans coming. We would have to run right away. They told us, "If the Germans are shooting, keep running and don't look back. Pray that they kill you instead of wounding you." Sometimes we started out with 25 or 30 people, and 10 or 15 would be gone.

AT ONE POINT, WE MET A MAN CARRYING A TORAH—not a small one, it had weight to it. He was exhausted and told my father he could no longer carry it. Zelik said, "It's okay. I'll take it. I'll carry it." We kept it safe during the whole war, in Siberia and everywhere we went. My father carried it, hid it, and kept it safe.

We drank water from puddles. We caught parasites in our stomachs and lice in our hair. Very little food, very cold and life was hell. There was no one to help us except God. So we kept praying and going on.

We had no books, no paper, and no pencils. My mother, mainly, re-

membered all the prayers by heart and we would just pray, silently or whatever, whatever we could. It wasn't something where you could be in a room
and study for awhile and have books and paper and literature. We had
nothing—no pictures, no papers. Later I tried to get my birth certificate,
but according to the government we were never born, my brothers and I.
There was no trace of any birth certificates for us.

This lasted until almost 1943. We were crossing rivers, going on little
dinghies to get across the Dvina River in Russia. The current was so strong
a few children would go first, and the parents later. But we did not know
when they put us in the little boat if we were going to see our parents again.
They were putting us on the other side where already the Russians were and
the Germans were on our heels. We did not know if they would catch our
parents and shoot them or not. You might not be able to see your parents
until an hour later. God was with us, because we always were able to find
them.

One time we were in the woods and we were wearing the same clothes
we had left the house with. Everything was raggedy, the shoes—everything
was torn. We literally looked like we didn't belong in this world. Like ghosts
in shreds, hanging. I think that God was with us or else we would not have
made it.

One time we were in the woods and I had to use the rest room, so you
would go behind trees where there were no people. And I remember like
today—I still keep dreaming about it, I kept walking and walking and
walking towards water. The trees were…you know when you're little, everything looks tall and big. I kept walking and walking. I was not getting
anywhere. I started praying and turned around, and I found my way back.

It was also a miracle from God that I made it.

And then one time we were caught in the woods and the woods were in the middle of an area occupied in White Russia. It was beginning to freeze and it was getting very cold and we didn't have any proper clothes. We were starving and shivering and all of a sudden we heard the Germans speak and the dogs barking. Our luck was that we were in an area where there was water and bushes. We went through the water up to our knees, and the dogs couldn't trace the smell. We had to sit like this all day long until nightfall, shivering in the cold frost—no food, no shelter—just by the cover of God and the trees.

I think when God does certain miracles with one hand,
you suffer and He can see you suffering—
He can't accept it —He looks away.
On the other hand, He was always with us
or we would not have made it.

I never had a cold, never got sick. The Germans would die before they could get to us. The Germans couldn't survive in that cold. We sat all day long like this, in the water, until the dark of night to cross high railroad tracks on a trestle about 15 or 20 feet higher than just a plain, flat railroad track. We were up to our necks in water and Zelik still had that Torah. How he kept it dry, I don't know. God must have helped. We survived the night in the water and so did the Torah. After the war was over, that Torah was donated in Akron, Ohio, but we don't know exactly where.

My older brother Herman didn't want to go on. He sat under a tree and he cried, "I'm not going. I don't care if the Germans catch me. I'm not going." He must've been 13 or 14. Edla begged him, but he wouldn't move. He said, "I don't care, let them kill me. I'm cold and hungry—I don't want to go." Edla took off her wedding band and gave it to one of the Partisans. He had a gun but what could he do against twenty Germans with their ammunition and everything? They took two branches, like the Indians would, and tied it across with something and dragged him on it like a sled for awhile. He was oldest, but he complained the most.

We got across that high trestle, and we wound up in the *Ural*—the coal mines, very rich in natural resources. It was very, very, very cold. When you walked the ground spoke to you, crunch, crunch, crunch. Some Jewish people from there came to see how they could help. They brought us a few pieces of bread and rags to wrap around our feet. When we were still deciding where to go, we were told they could send us either to Tashkent, Uzbekistan, Pakistan, or Siberia. My father was learned in many things, but he didn't know the geography of the world. They told him Siberia was very, very cold and hard. We were about 150 kilometers from the North Pole, so you could imagine. We didn't have warm clothes, we were not well-fed or well sheltered. They told us that in Tashkent, it's very, very, very hot.

I remember it like today, Zelik looking at Edla, and he called her Mamaleh, like Mommy, and he said, "I think we should go to Siberia, because if we go to Tashkent, we're going to die from malaria, from dysentery, cholera, from diseases. In Siberia we will starve, we'll freeze but so will the lice and so will the germs." He called it *chaleris*, bad things. Up until then we didn't have colds, we didn't get sick. Even the lice that we had, they froze too. A lot of people went to Tashkant, and they died. They lived in very tight quarters. The sanitation was very, very poor and so was the food and medical.

To get to Siberia, we were going to get on a train, but the train got bombed. So we had to be in ditches for weeks again, in the middle of nowhere. We finally made it on another train, and the good thing about Siberia was we didn't have to lock the door or be afraid that anybody would come to kill us. The people were nice and friendly and they called us *bieznitsi* or refugees. We went to live on a collective farm and we lived in a stall with a horse for a whole year.

My parents knew how to work on a farm, so my father started feeding the horses, going to cut wood in the forest. The people who lived there had a tremendous advantage over my father. They had shoes made from lamb's wool; they would take the skin and make a coat and a hood and put the wool on the inside and the skin on the outside. They called them *volinki*, and they wore big gloves up to here. The people made vodka out of potatoes, so when they came to work in 40-below zero, they didn't feel the cold. My father had thin shoes with rags and newspapers wrapped around them. He didn't have gloves, so he used rags to wrap around his hands.

My mother would milk the cows and feed the pigs. We survived by stealing a little milk from the cows, and eating food meant for the pigs. She would wake up at two or three in the morning, and milk a little from each cow's teat. If she took too much, somebody would know the milk was taken out, and it would be really bad to get caught stealing. We'd each have a little glass of milk. It was like manna from heaven, to sustain us.

My younger brother and I went to school every single day in rags. People would sometimes be kind and give us extra rags. Edla sewed clothes, so if there was a little something left over, she would combine it and make a blouse for me. The teacher felt sorry for me, and she would let me sit by the hot water heater to dry my feet because I would have frozen toes. Another girl was jealous of me. She called me a dirty Jew and tormented me. I told my mother, who spoke to the teacher. The girl was disciplined but she didn't stop. One day we were in the school yard and she did it again. I looked down and there was a big rock. When she said, "Dirty Jew," I picked up the rock and slammed her in the head with it. She didn't bother me again and I didn't get in trouble. I learned sometimes the only person who can stand up for you is you. I was very small, but I learned to take care of myself. It's called survival.

David on the bicycle given to him by UNRRA. He was a messenger. 1946

I WAS A VERY GOOD STUDENT even though I had only one outfit of clothes. I was always clean and I was hungry to learn, so I never missed a day. The minute the snow would fall, it would turn like an ice cube. While I went to school we lived with that horse in his stall for a whole winter.

It was during this time that my little sister Sara was born on February 27th. It was a blessed day of happiness for us all when she arrived happy and healthy.

My brother Herman had a job to fill a barrel with water and take it to the bakery. He had a sled with a horse and a barrel like a wine or beer barrel, with a hole in it. He would take big buckets from the well and fill up the barrel. His hands and face would freeze while he did this job. Then he would take the water to the bakery, and they would wash the pots clean of dough. The doughy water was brought back to give to the pigs. Bran that they sifted out when they sifted the flour was floating on the top of the water, also for the pigs. My mother made up a little bag to put around my brother's neck, and the minute he left the bakery, he would stop and grab the bran before it got soaked, and put it in the little bag. Edla would make us little pancakes out of it.

Also at the bakery, bread in the oven would rise over the top, and little pieces would fall to the bottom of the oven. That was collected for the pigs, too. That's what we survived on—food collected for the pigs and milk Edla got from the cows at night.

A monument erected in Myadel, Poland to honor those first murdered when the Germans arrived. Picture taken 2004. "In memory of the Jews of Myadel who were murdered by German Nazis and their collaborators 1941–45 in Myadel and its surroundings, in the forests near Kamina and Usaci on the battlefront and with the Partisans."

DAVID REMEMBERS WARTIME

In 1939, the Germans came and occupied our city. They ordered all the Jewish people to wear a yellow band with a Star of David. They put us on a curfew, and gave us ration cards because they closed up almost all the Jewish stores and businesses. If you wanted bread, even though the bakery stayed the same and baked bread for the Germans as well, you could only get so much bread. You had to bring your ration card. After awhile, they created a ghetto. A certain section was called Kamionka, where there was a hilly, stoney area. All the Jews had to get out of their homes, leave all their belongings and go and live in the ghetto, in assigned living quarters.

My grandmother Reizel had the good fortune not to be tortured by the Nazis, because she passed away soon after the Germans came in. My father was able to inter her remains and she was buried in Bedin.

A year later the Germans created *Judenrein*. The word means "clean of Jews." They made demands that people show up in a certain place, like a big field, and they delegated and segregated and chose who went to Auschwitz or concentration camps. The Germans also created a Jewish city hall. They took certain Jews and made them work. They gave them orders, such as, "Tomorrow, send 400

David, a year after liberation. 1946

Jewish people to be designated as to where they're going." It wasn't an easy task because those people had to choose which names to give to the Germans. They appointed a Jewish police force. I was chosen a few times to be shipped here or there, but every time, I was lucky. I didn't go straight.

Then they created a liquidation camp in our city. My family was chosen to be in that camp, and all the people that they chose, hid out in the ghetto. My family hid in the attic of a small apartment building. My grandfather hid in the basement below, because we couldn't all be in the attic. There were two families. One day, we had some potatoes that somebody sneaked up and word got out. The Gestapo came and threw us down. One thing I'll never forget as long as I live…they caught my dear grandfather, Menachem Mendel Koplowicz. He was in the cellar below in the same building, and I heard the Germans say, "Lauf, lauf, lauf. You there, Jew, run, run, run." Menachem loudly pronounced, "Hear O Israel, the Lord our God, the Lord is One." He recited the Shema. And BOOM, I heard a shot and my grandfather, Menachem, fell dead. I never saw him again.

When we came to the liquidation camp, my father, Kople, was sent to a work detail. I was left in the camp, and an SS officer wanted me to take care of his horse—to brush the horse.

Entertaining himself, he took out his pistol and shot a cat out of my hand. When Kople came back from the work detail, my mother, Brajndla, and my sister Pearl, six years old, had already been taken away and I haven't seen them since. Of course, I heard all kinds of things, but who knows?

Kople came back from the work detail, and he had a little bottle of poison in his pocket that he was going to take if he didn't find any of us. I was still there, so he tried to go for my mother and sister but they stopped him.

They said if he went, he would never come back, and they didn't know what would happen to me. So he stayed.

In the liquidation camp, Kople grew a big moustache. There were some friends who arranged to get a pair of leather boots for me. It was arranged that my father and I would run away from the camp. My father gave the money that he had, and whatever he had that was valuable, to get help. We ran away from Bedin to Katowice. There, we hooked up with an Aryan family whose son was a Gestapo hiding out with us in the cellar, too. From Bedin to Katowice, you had to go by train or some type of transportation. I had these boots and I had a Hitler Juden (Hitler Youth) brown uniform. I was taught how to say, God forgive me, "Heil Hitler."

David and Kople, in their apartment outside the Displaced Persons Camp, Landsberg am Lech.1946-47

We got there and hid, for about three months or less. There was a lightbulb that had markings on it—painted somehow, so that if somebody came to the door, we knew to keep quiet. A few times the Gestapo came to search the house because somebody snitched that they were hiding Jews. One day the son, who was a Gestapo that was hiding with us, decided we all had to get out of there or we would be caught.

A plan was arranged. First, we had to go to the railroad station, then on a truck to run away from Poland to Czechoslovakia. There was a lot of sleeping in the back of a big church or synagogue. I remember walking over big, big hills. From there, we crossed the border to Hungary. Again, some guides that were paid very well, took us to the main synagogue in Bratislava where the statue, the famous Golem, is made out of clay. That's a very famous piece of history.

From Bratislava, we went to Hungary, crossing mountains on foot. Guides smuggled us across the border. They left us in the Dóhany Utcai Zsinagóga. In English, it's now called the Budapest Great Synagogue.

Again, somebody snitched because the guides didn't come back for us. The police came and arrested us. My father and I were supposed to get papers from Hungary that we were not Jewish—that we were Aryan, and to be put in a place where we could live through the war in Hungary without being sent to a concentration camp. But that didn't work for us. Why didn't it work? Because the person in charge of giving those papers to us was away on a fling with his mistress and he wasn't going to come back for four more days or so. So we wound up in the Budapest jail. My father was on one side and I was on the other with a bunch of rough gang guys and some of the very beautiful curse words that I learned, I haven't forgotten to this day. I learned some Hungarian, which I still remember.

From there, we were put into a detention facility in Budapest for about two or three months and shipped to a camp called Garain. There were Jews, there were non-Jews. There was a man by the name of Gayza Bluestein who

David dresses for a play, in character as an American soldier, Displaced Persons Camp. 1946–47

was a violinist and played beautifully.

The wife of the camp *commandant* was standing in her kitchen when her maid yelled out, "Bluestein…do you want a piece of cake?" So Bluestein says, "If I want a piece of cake, I will go to the head…I don't ask the ass." And the wife brought him out half a cake. He said to me, "Don't you forget…if you learn this, you will live through this war. Never go to the ass, always go to the head." I will die remembering that.

THAT MAN GAVE ME COURAGE. He taught me a lot of things. He wanted to teach me violin, but I didn't want to learn. Again came a day when the Germans decided that all Hungarian Jews were going to be shipped to Auschwitz, Majdanek, Treblinka. My father and I were part of that and they shipped us from Garain, where they took out all the Jews, and took us by train to Shatra Uynell, where they put us in cattle cars to ship us to Germany. After all that, we wound up being sent back to the place we ran away from.

The Hungarian Jews didn't believe my father and I that we were going to a death camp. They said, "Oh come on, what are you talking about?

Yiddish Theatre Group, Displaced Persons Camp. David, top right. 1947

We're going to a work camp." They took their bedcovers, their down covers, their sewing machines and finally we arrived in Auschwitz and they started emptying the wagons. Adolf Eichmann, whom you have heard about, was segregating to the left, the work detail and other camp assignments; to the right, women, children, or they chose certain women for work and other women, you'll pardon the expression, for prostitution and worse. The children were going straight to the crematorium and gas chambers.

In front of the officers, I clicked my heels and said, "Sir, I am a carpenter, I'm 18 years of age and I'm able to work." I lied. Kople was near me and we locked arms. The officer said, *"Links,"* (left) and so we stayed together. Then, of all things, I was bitten by a German Shepherd dog.

THERE WAS ONE YOUNG FELLOW who was chosen to go to the crematorium. They put him on a truck and he jumped off and ran away. They thought that I was that young man. So they put me in the truck, and I jumped three times. I was saved by a man who was an artist, a sculptor. He made sculptings of heads. He told the Nazis, "This is my child, and I will sculpt for you and work for you, if you leave my son." So, I came before the "big shot," once again, and said I was 18, a carpenter, and able to work. He said, "Links." And again, I locked arms with my father and three others, and the next thing I knew, thank God, they didn't take us to the crematorium, but they issued us concentration camp suits—white with blue stripes—and wooden clogs. They shaved our heads right down the middle and cut off almost all our hair.

I was lucky. I don't have any numbers burned into me. I did not receive a tattoo. In Auschwitz, they were so packed, that they had to send us to sub-camps from there. So I received a number on a piece of linen. I don't remember the number. It was sewn onto my concentration camp uniform.

From there, I went to Kittlitztreben. I was there until the end of 1944, or a little before. The Russians were coming our way, so the Germans liquidated the camp and we were marched on foot to Buchenwald. People died like flies on the way. Some of them were shot. If they didn't get shot, they were beaten to death. Not too many people survived. It didn't matter how tall you were, how robust you were, how strong you were—nobody could survive this kind of life. As far as I'm concerned, it was God's will as to who survived it. People were dying of hunger, of exposure, of exhaustion, lice, sickness. There was no medicine, there was nothing. You laid there and you either survived or you didn't.

Once we were on a farm where we slept in the barns and before marching away from that farm, a pregnant woman wanted to give me some milk and bread. When I say pregnant, she was very pregnant. The German soldier hit her with the butt of the rifle in her stomach and hit me over the head because she wanted to give me some food.

I was in the Kittlitztreben work camp, and the SS was the main leader of the camp. And there was a German who was like a political prisoner. His name was Otto, and he had murdered women, but he liked children. I was the alarm clock, with five other boys, singing for him all kinds of songs to wake him up and serenade him. Once or twice a year, he gave us a little extra soup, or milk, or soup with noodles. The man was not fit for society, but yet he had power. At the same time, he had some decency in him. They almost shipped me to a concentration camp where I was going to go to the crematorium, and he saved my life by putting a pillow inside my pants and taking a whip to me. He said, "When I lower the whip, I want you to scream like hell." He saved my life by pretending to beat me badly, and it saved me from going to the other camp, Gross-Rosen.

Wermacht soldiers dug up a couple of potatoes from the field with the bayonets on their rifles, and gave them to me. Once they gave me flapjacks. They knew that my father was with me in the camp and I brought some of the flapjacks home. Home...listen to me, home, I mean the barracks, to share with my father, Kople. You can forgive, but you cannot forget. How can you forget?

The liberation of Buchenwald happened on April 11, 1945, when an American tank crashed through the fence. The Army infantry 1st and 6th divisions liberated us under General Dwight D. Eisenhower. When General Eisenhower came, I escorted him to where the naked, dead bodies were, and showed him the pile of skeletons.

At the liberation, when the Americans came in, I still had my head shaved in the middle. There was just the skin because there was no hair there. And there were a lot of African-Americans that liberated us and they looked at me, because I was so sunburned and dark and dirty, and said, "Look, look, look." They thought I was African. I didn't mind. They gave me some chocolate and cigarettes. I gave the cigarettes to Kople because my father was a heavy smoker.

Kople was sick with typhus at the time of the liberation, and I was able to somehow organize a couple of eggs, which I boiled. I made the eggs with raw onion for Kople and took them to the barrack to save his life because he needed something to eat. When he saw me bringing eggs to him, he was so happy. To this day, eggs with onions are one of my favorite foods to remember, because I did something for my Dad, and he so appreciated his eggs with the yellow soft and whole, and the white of the eggs mixed in. That's one of my memories.

Our American liberators cooked beef stew for those that had survived. Of course, everybody started grabbing and eating, but people had dysentery, their digestive tracts were starving and couldn't handle heavy food, and some of them died. They should've been given a little crumbled egg and milk because heavy greasy food is too much after everything has shriveled up inside of you. But nobody knew that then. They meant well.

Kople recovered from typhus and gained his strength back, but we did not have the will to go back to Poland to see where we lost our entire family, so we shipped to a displaced persons' camp. I spoke some English and German, as well as other languages, and I began to work for the UNRRA, United Nations Relief and Rehabilitation Administration. I was given the privilege of becoming a messenger and worked myself up from there. I got to wear an American uniform with the UNRRA insignia. That was a big deal then and I got a bicycle to run around on. I was so lucky that I drove it into a trash truck and ran my head into a barrel. But, I managed.

Later on, I tried to become an electrician and I held on to a big electric wire which threw me down. That was the end of the electrician's job. I wanted to learn how to box. A guy punched me right in the nose and my nose was bleeding like crazy, so that was the end of my boxing career. I should've gone into a conservatory, but I went to work with the AJDC—the American Joint Distribution Committee, which was formed by a philanthropic organization in the United States to help survivors normalize again. I had a co-worker and we drove around to DP camps, showing films on a projector to survivors. That's where I met my wife for the first time, although I had no idea. Some little girls came over to the projector, and Yetta was one of them. She was too young for me to be interested in her at the time, just a girl of fourteen. But I remembered her. I remembered her very, very distinctly.

I met Leonard Bernstein in Munich. He came to Germany, performing concerts for displaced people. He had a lady pianist and I drove with them and took him around.

From there, I got to work for the USDPC—United States Displaced Persons' Commission. I was part of the CIA and I was already an Interpreter. When people came to be chosen to go to the United States, I would translate and interpret who should be able to come into the United States and who shouldn't. Not that I made the decision, but I was the Interpreter for the Commission.

People thought I must be a very, very rich fellow because I helped a lot of people get their visas to America. They thought I was taking money for doing that. I didn't take a nickel. When I worked for the AJDC, I met a man who brought us to the United States. His name was Ben Solnit, and he was a very rich man. He owned a shoe factory and a wholesale shoe house in Los Angeles. He told me that he would like to sponsor me to come to the United States. I was able to come through the Hebrew Immigration Aid

Society, but I chose to take him up on it; he was a multimillionaire.

Why did I do it that way? It's like a fellow comes during the depression to Rothschild and wants that he should lend him a thousand dollars. Of course, the Rothschilds do not lend out money just like that. Rothschild says "I'll tell you what. If you come back tomorrow I'll take a little walk with you and you'll get all the money that you want." So, the next day Rothschild puts his arm around the fellow's shoulder as they walk down Wall Street. Rothschild says, "Go into this bank and you're going to get anything you want." So, sure enough, the bankers see he's walking down the street with Rothschild, and he got the loan and everything he wanted. It depends who you walk with.

Shabbat challah tray and knife.

I said to Mr. Solnit that I wanted very much to take him up on his sponsorship to America, but I had a problem: if he wanted to bring me, he had to bring my father too. He said okay and brought us both. Ben and Bertha Solnit. Bless them. Kople went to work for them in the shoe factory, and I worked in the shoe wholesale house. Kople and I were only in the country two weeks before we went to work. Dad was proud and wouldn't take any charity or things from organizations that offered us. He felt we were both well enough to work, and work would make us stronger. My father was right, of course.

David's beloved English teacher, Marie Kilbride, 1950. David says, "My English is better today because of her."

Chapter Three
Coming to America

David

I came here on May 19, 1949, on a ship called the UST Marine Marlin. It used to be an Army ship. Before the end of May I was already working—for 55 cents an hour for Mr. Solnit who sponsored me. He was a very charitable man, a philanthropist. I registered at Roosevelt High School, and studied in the evenings. At the end of 1949, I received my high school diploma.

I had a teacher by the name of Marie Kilbride and she set me on vocabulary, vocabulary, vocabulary. There was a very pretty young woman sitting next to me in class, and Mrs. Kilbride must have thought that I was more interested in exchanging conversation than school work. She called me up to the front of the room and said, "When you come back, you sit here each time, and you bring twenty words on three-by-five cards, with the spelling of the word, what the word means, and how to pronounce it. And come a half hour early each time or you're out of this class." Well, let me tell you something, may God rest her soul, she really did me the biggest favor. Because when I went to City College, I earned the name of Walking Dictionary.

I met Mitzi Gaynor there, one of the top singing and dancing movie stars of her time, before she became famous. Mitzi was from Hungary, but she wasn't Jewish.

When we came to the United States, we were two poor kids. I started my job as a stock clerk at the Solnit Shoe Company and then I became a shipping clerk and I got 75 cents an hour. Then I had the audacity to quit and go across the street and get a job for $1.05 an hour.

Yetta

As soon as I came to the United States in 1949, I had to go to school for 10 hours a week before I could get a permit to work, because it was a financial hardship on my parents. I have a cousin, Minnie, who is now 94, and she was the one who taught me about work and how to find jobs. Her mother, Aunt Dora, sponsored us to America, and she had to hock her house so that we would not have to go on government subsidy. A lot of friends were worried about her giving the house up as collateral. My father went to work right away as a dishwasher. He had never washed a dish before in his life. He was a businessman back in Poland, but he couldn't do it yet in America because he didn't speak English.

My first job was on Los Angeles Street, and it was about 85 or 90 degrees in there. I'm just here from Europe—I don't speak a word of English. I'm put in a factory where there are mostly African-American women, most of them were very tall and very large and they perspired a lot. They were spitting in a coffee can, chewing tobacco or whatever. I weighed about 98 pounds at the time. It was my first time to see African-American people, except for pictures in a book. I used to come home crying because I was petrified all the time. It was hot, very stuffy and very foreign to me, and they all looked at me like I came out of a zoo. Here was this little kid, with blonde Shirley Temple curls. I wasn't even 16, but I had a permit to work.

From there, my cousin Minnie, Aunt Lena's daughter, found me a job at Charm Fit of Hollywood on Bundy and Olympic in Santa Monica. They weren't going to hire me, but I came for the interview, and I was dressed very neatly and orderly. I already spoke some English—but not a lot. The gentleman who interviewed me was a prince of a man. He was an Irishman and he sees I'm very young. I told him I could sew, that I took sewing and designing, and I had a diploma. He looked at me and looked at me, trying to figure out

what nationality I was. He said, "What's your nationality?" I said, "I'm Polish." He didn't ask me my religion—just my nationality. If he would have asked me my religion, I would have told him that I was Jewish.

So he hired me. The owners were German Jews; they were Reform. They had a niece who worked for them and was able to speak German, so I had no problem. There was a lady and a man who spoke Russian to me. The forelady made me an assistant to the designer. I sewed up samples for her. They were always perfect. We used to make bras for Zsa Zsa Gabor, Ava

Left to right: Aunt Dora, Edla, Sara, Zelik, Yetta. Aunt Dora put her house up for collateral so the family could come to America.

Gardner, all the movie stars. In those days, one little bra would cost $50 or $60 dollars, and a dollar a yard for lace, so you had to be very careful. We're talking 60 years ago, so they were very expensive.

My mom would give me just enough money for carfare, so I would take a piece of fruit and a sandwich, or whatever, and that was that. I worked through the lunch hour and through the breaks. While they were standing and smoking and drinking coffee and gossiping, I was working. When the Jewish holidays were coming around, I told my boss I was sorry but I could not come in on those days. He said, "Why not?" I said, "Because I am Jewish. I cannot work on those holidays." He said, "Well, you didn't tell us you were Jewish." I said, "You didn't ask me. You asked me my nationality and I told you I was born in Poland."

I worked piecework and made $100 a week. Sometimes more than that, $150. A lawyer didn't make any more than that.

Yetta, bottom right, with other children on a kibbutz in
Germany. 1946–47

January 19th, 1952. Outside it was raining cats and dogs, but the sun was shining in our hearts.

Chapter Four
A wedding to remember

Yetta

It was nine or ten months before David's discharge from the Army, so we planned on having a wedding. My parents didn't have any money and my father was working for $50 a week. My mother, Edla, said that we would make a wedding at their little shul. It would hold about 60 people, most of our relatives, and we would have honey cake and sponge cake and some wine and nuts and raisins and garbanzo beans. The Rabbi would perform the ceremony and we would be married, and it would all cost between $50 and $75. I told my mother thank you, we really appreciated it, but I wanted to have a regular wedding. I asked them, if they didn't mind, that for the next three or four months, I would not give them my wages, like I usually did. If it was okay, I would save my money to pay for the wedding. They said that was fine.

The Wedding. Left to right: Helen, Kople, Lena, Sanford, Malah Langholz, Edla, Yetta and David.

I went to Temple Beth Am, on La Cienega, and told them we were newcomers and my fiancé was in the Army, and we would like to get married there. They said that first we had to be members and then it would cost $300 for the shul and everything. I said we didn't have the money to be members plus $300 and that was the end of that.

David was singing for Betty Burke at Park Manor and she treated him like a grandson. She was about 65 or 70 years old and was a beautiful lady and loved David. She said, "I will make you kids a beautiful wedding and charge you only $3.50 per person. We had appetizers, stuffed cabbage, meatballs, soup, roasted chicken, soup, strudel—we had everything, you name it. In those days, it may have been $7.50 per person, but for David, it was $3.50.

The day of the wedding on January 19th, 1952, there was wind, rain coming down, mud everywhere. We had about 150 people at the wedding and Rabbi Paul Dubin came to marry us. But he was coming through Paso Robles and it was extremely flooded. He called to tell us to have all the festivities first, eat the food, have a good time, and then, when he arrived, we would have the ceremony last. That's the way it went and we had a beautiful wedding and we just celebrated our 59th wedding anniversary.

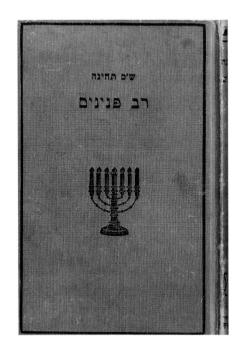

תְּחִנָּה מוֹדֶה אֲנִי

מוֹדֶה אֲנִי לְפָנֶיךָ, נָאם מֵין נָאמ און נָאמ פון מַיְנֶע עֶלְ־
טֶערֶען, אִיךְ אָרֶימֶע פְרוֹי שְׁטֶעהֶע פַאר דִיר מִיט אָן
אַיְינְגֶעבּוֹיגֶענֶעם קאפ, מִיט אַ צוּבְּרָאכֶען הַארְץ, דֶען מַיְין
לֶעבֶּען אִיז אִין דַיְין האַנְד און מַיְין טוֹים אִיז אוֹיךְ אִין דַיְין
האַנְד. אִיךְ שְׁטֶעהֶע פַאר דִיר מִיט לוֹיטֶער צִיטֶערְנִישׁ. אִיךְ
בֶּאנְגֶעהֶר פוּן דִיר, אַז דוּ זָאלְסְט מִיר מוֹחֵל זַיין מַיְנֶע זִינְד וָואס
אִיךְ הָאבּ גֶעזִינְדִיגְט און גֶעשׁוּלְדִיגְט פוּן דֶעם מָאג פוּן מַיְין
גֶעבּוּרְט בִּיז הַיְינְטִיגֶען טָאג, און אוֹיבּ אִיךְ הָאבּ גֶעזִינְדִיגְט
אִין דִי דָרַיי מִצְוֹת וָואס דִי הָאקסְט גֶעבָּאטֶען אונְז וַוייבֶּער,
חַלָה, נִדָה און לִיכְט־צִינְדֶען, בֶּעט אִיךְ דִיךְ, אַז דוּ זָאלְסְט
מִיר הַיְינְט דָאס נִיט גֶעדֶענְקֶען און אִין חָלִילָה מַיְנֶע יָאהְרֶען נִיט
אָפְּשְׁנַיידֶען, נָאר דוּ זָאלְסְט מִיךְ נָאךְ לָאזֶען לֶעבֶּען בִּיז אִיךְ
וֶועל מְקַיֵים זַיין וָואס עֶס שְׁטֶעהְטוּ אִין דַיְין תּוֹרָה, און וֶוען מַיְין
צַיְיט וֶועט קוּמֶען צוּ שְׁטַארְבֶּען, זָאל דִי מִיתָה זַיין אַ כַּפָּרָה
אוֹיף מַיְנֶע זִינְד, אֲפִילוּ אִיךְ הָאבּ דָאס נִיט פַערְדִינְט בַּיי
דַיְין לֶעבֶּען נָאמֶען, בֶּעט אִיךְ דִיךְ אַ מַתְּנַת חִנָם, דוּ הָערְסְט
דָאם גֶעבֶּעט פוּן אַלֶע מֶענְשֶׁען, זָאלְסְטוּ אוֹיךְ הֶערֶען מַיְין גֶע־
בֶּעט, אָמֵן, כֵּן יְהִי רָצוֹן:

אָנָּא הַשֵׁם, אִיךְ בֶּעט דִיךְ נָאם און נָאם פון מַיְנֶע עֶלְ־

התעוררות פאר דער תפלה

עֶר אִיז אַרוֹים פון בֵּית־הַכְּנֶסֶת (שׁוּל) │ נָאכְדֶעם אוֹי וַוייט שׁוֶועלְכֶען פַאר אִים
און קָאם גֶעמֶאנְקְט אַז וֶועדֶער זָאל אִים │ מִיט הַכְּנָסָה, מִיט נָרוֹת בֶּעזוֹנֶיין און
אוֹיפְגֶעבֶּען צוּ בֶּענְטְשֶׁען, דָאם צְרָ־כֶע │ שְׁלֶעכְטֶעם וַוייל, און וֶועדֶער וַוייטֶער און
מָעהֶען אַז הוּנְגֶערֶענְדֶער מֶענְשֶׁען פון │ קְלָיְדֶען, אַז עֶר זָאל אִים מִשְׁפָּט

Edla's wedding gift to Yetta: a book of women's prayers called Rav Pninim, in Hebrew, meaning Great Precious Pearls of Wisdom. Also called Tzena Rena in Yiddish. Left: the Modeh Ani prayer. This is the Hebrew prayer recited upon awakening, thanking God for returning one's soul.

Edla's inscription to Yetta inside the front cover of her wedding gift. "A remembrance from your beloved mother. You should not hide it or put it away. You should hold it dear, and when you hold it in your hands, you will remember me, your mother. Hold it lovingly, my child."

The rabbi's tallit. A close-up of the fabric and the crown, fashioned from sterling silver, and hand-sewn into a collar for the garment. A gift from Edla, the rabbi's mother-in-law, blessed memory, upon his ordination.

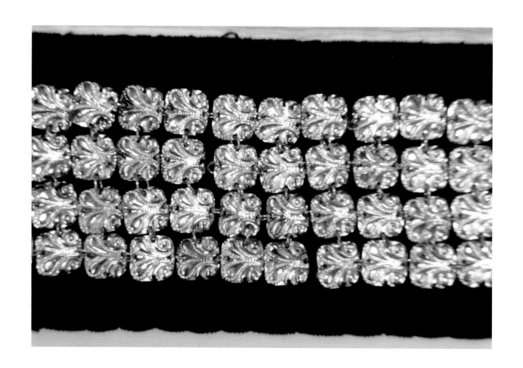

A close-up of the tallit's silver crown.

Early Married Life

Yetta

After the wedding, we got our first apartment off of Highland Avenue, near Olympic Boulevard in Los Angeles. We had the will and desire to better ourselves. We worked full time and studied until three and four in the morning. We got up at 7:00 A.M. after sleeping only three or four hours. When David was studying, I was cooking and asking him questions, checking on the spelling, checking on the answers. I would ask a question from the book, and he would answer it and correct it.

The G.I. Bill paid for David's education and he was getting $175 per month from the government for going to college. He got all the books for free. The apartment wasn't elegant, but it was spotless. I started cooking for Shabbat on Thursday night. I did all the cooking for Friday, Saturday and Sunday. On Sunday I started cooking for Monday through Thursday and then I started all over again. I made my own noodles. I rolled them out and dried them on the tablecloth.

We used to go with my parents, Edla and Zelik, to a farm in La Puente and buy 50 or 60 chickens. We used to take the *shochet*, the ritual slaughterer with us. We would pay him ten cents a head and feed him. We paid 16 cents a pound for fresh chicken, and a whole-body chicken for $1.50. We would bring it home, pluck out all the feathers, open it, separate the liver, the gizzard, the neck. Just like we used to do on the farm as a child. I would salt the meat and soak it. When it was kosher, we would dry it and wrap it in freezer paper. We rented a locker at the university to store it. We had chicken every way that chicken could be made and it was delicious.

We got along on a very, very limited budget, but we always had enough for everything. Today, people buy things that they can't pay for. If we didn't have the money, we didn't buy it. Whatever we bought, we paid for, and paid our bills two days before they were due. We didn't go to the movies, theatre, anything. All we did was work and save. Later, when we made our money and had it saved, we traveled the world.

David and TV talent show host, Horace Heidt. David won $150 for singing *Eli Eli* in Hebrew.

David

I was a shipping clerk and one day I lifted a heavy case. I hurt my back a little and Yetta said, "You're quitting tomorrow. You're not going to work there anymore. You have a G.I. Bill coming, so you're going to college." I registered at Los Angeles City College and two years later I had an Associate Arts degree. I am very grateful to the United States and the Army that they paid for my college. I continued with a minor in music and a major in accounting.

Then I registered at the Los Angeles State College, now known as the University of Los Angeles and got my Bachelor of Science Degree in the accountancy program. Debbie Reynolds, who became a famous film star and the mother of Carrie Fisher, went to school there too. I also studied for my cantorate and rabbinate. I got my first full-time position in the cantorate in late 1953 at the Alhambra Synagogue Center in Alhambra, California. I used to take voice lessons and pay as much as $50 a lesson. We didn't have a couch to sit on, but we had money for a voice lesson. One fellow was a tremendous pianist and voice teacher Noel Cravat. My teachers were accomplished musicians as well as good voice teachers

At the time, artistry was not cheap. It's one of the things Yetta and I appreciate in life because of the suffering we went through. Like my wife said, "We went from hell to paradise."

I got a job with Rashba-Pokard & Green in 1956. They're not there anymore. I got a job as a junior accountant and worked with them for not quite two years until I was laid off because they had too many junior accountants. So I got a job with Shanken & McGuigen. After income tax season, I didn't have a job, so I worked for Mr. Maurice Newman, a certificate #36, CPA in California. He was a very brilliant man despite diabetes and a speech impediment.

I did the books and the accounting for Mr. Newman and one day I was sent to a yardage store on Los Angeles Street belonging to Mickey Cohen's sister. Mickey Cohen, I might remind you, was one of the most notorious mobsters who ever lived. In 1961 he was sentenced to 15 years in Alcatraz prison for tax evasion. They couldn't catch him any other way. So back to my story, a big black limousine drives up to the curb and guys come out and then Mickey Cohen comes out and says, "Hi kid, what is this—they send kids?" He said, "How ya doin' kid?" Someone whispers, "Do you know who this is? It's Mickey Cohen." I don't know if he took a liking to me, but he patted me on the head and I was "in." The other thing is, his sister had a store because of him. He was backing her.

I got into more things—I traded, I bartered with a kosher butcher and did his books and he gave me kosher meat. I was a salesman at the same time as I studied and completed my cantorate. I went into selling burial plans for Mount Sinai Memorial Park. At that time they didn't have computers and they didn't have a presentation with a computer so I had to flip pages. One man didn't want me to use my presentation. He said, "Don't take it out." Okay, okay I didn't take it out. But we talked and talked and I convinced him. I said, "You wouldn't want your wife to have to pick out a plot or arrange for a funeral. You want to protect your family." Anyway, he made out a check. At the last minute, his wife said to me, "By the way, I want to pay for a casket—a paper casket. I want to tear off a piece of it!" Yetta was sitting with the kids in the car for almost three hours waiting. I came out and made over $2,000 on the sale. That was in 1954–55.

I had a very, very interesting learning process. I could say that outside of my university training, I went to the "hard knock school." Once I stopped in Boyle Heights at around 10:30 at night where five old men were playing cards. I knocked on the door and asked them if I could come in. When they found out what I wanted, I said, "Listen, I have kids at home and my wife is waiting for me and I haven't made a sale today. Please won't you let me in and let me tell you about it?" So one man bought and I wound up selling all five. It took guts for me to knock on the door and to tell them I was selling plots and a burial program. Once a woman told me that the crypt wasn't big enough for a person to be interned in it. I put down my satchel and climbed into the crypt to show her it was big enough. She almost fainted.

In 1957, I got my rabbinical ordination, so you can see that I didn't sleep too much...just go and go and go and study. Yetta encouraged me every step of the way. I also attended Chapman College for some psychology courses.

You have to know where you want to go and what you want to accomplish and go after it. As we say in our faith, in the Shema V'havta:

You shall love the Lord your God with all your heart,
and with all your soul, and with all your might.

And so, whatever you do, whatever you undertake to do, you have to do it with fervor.

Yemenite Hamsah, a blessing for the house.

Newlyweds at Fort Ord

Yetta

Rabbi Paul Dubin and his wife, Esther, may they rest in peace, invited us to their home in Ford Ord for a steak dinner. Such kind people to us. David was Paul's assistant chaplain on the base. There was *bloteh*, which is Yiddish for mud, up to your knees because it was a new housing area for the officers. There were no streets and we could barely get in.

Like mother, like daughter. Yetta and Edla, full of joy, at Fort Ord. 1953

We were there for nine months and those were the best nine months for newlyweds—nobody there to bother us. There was no danger of David being sent overseas because he had too little time left in the Army for them to send him overseas and bring him back. We lived off-base in a beautiful apartment—a converted garage in the back of a bar. We could hear the soldiers when they would come out drinking. I was petrified. I was 18, a month away from my 19th birthday. We would put a dresser by the door every night in case somebody tried to break in. We paid $60 a month rent—that included everything. The only thing extra was the telephone.

We got our kosher meat from Los Angeles. My mother would put it on the bus, packed in ice, on the Blue Line. We would go and meet the bus when it came in. We would order meat together with the Dubins, because they kept kosher, too. Sometimes Edla sent it a few times by airplane. Once in a

David's ordination by Dr. Rabbi Henach Singer, July, 1957.

while when we couldn't get it from Los Angeles, we got it from San Francisco.

At the PX on the base, we got canned kosher meats. In English, they call it Spam, but it was kosher. It looked like liverwurst. We went to the movies for 50 cents. The pay was $125 a month. Nobody was able to get a job back then, but I got a job because I knew how to sew. I did alterations in camp and sewed on stars and stripes. There were dozens and dozens of soldiers' wives answering telephones, but nobody knew how to sew. I made 65 cents an hour and was doing well. We had a little dog, but when I left him in the yard one day, somebody stole the dog. They opened the gate and took him. That was our loss, but we had a lot of friends there.

We went on the 17-mile drive in Monterey. There was nothing but trees on one side and sandy beach on the other side. We also used to go the stables and rent horses. I was very good on a horse from my experience as a child riding Sierkah, without a saddle.

We didn't drink, so we would sit down on the waterfront and hear the waves, and drink tea or coffee. We'd laugh and talk with three or four other couples and then go home. We didn't have much—we didn't need much. On Shabbat, I would invite a couple of the soldiers and every Friday night, David would arrange to go to Salinas for Shabbat services. All of a sudden, everybody became Jewish. They wanted to go because they met girls, and got served refreshments. We'd go in a car or a van, or a small bus. A couple of the young men met some nice, young ladies and got married. It was very, very beautiful. We were there for a year and a half.

The wedding. Left to right: Yetta, David, Rabbi Paul (Pinkie) Dubin and his wife, Esther.

Alhambra and Monterey Park

Yetta

When we came back to Los Angeles, David went to work and back to school and I went back to work at Charm Fit of Hollywood. It was a beautiful place—lovely people. I worked there until I was expecting our daughter, Bryna. December 25th there was a Christmas party and they told me I couldn't work anymore because they didn't want me to have the baby at work. They told me anytime I wanted to come back, I could stay there for life. They liked me.

I had enough saved for a washing machine, to pay the doctor and pay the hospital bill. In those days, that's how it worked. Today, first you accumulate the bills—then if you don't have the money, you don't have to pay.

When our daughter was born, I didn't go back to work. David worked at the Alhambra Synagogue Center with Rabbi Yosef Miller, may he rest in peace. Rabbi Miller got a job at Temple Beth Shalom in Long Beach in 1962, and he encouraged my husband to come with him. Already we had Bryna and Berry. Jerry was born later.

With the two children, we lived in Monterey Park. We had a lovely, brand new home and got it on the G.I. Bill. We paid two and a half percent interest, $165 per month. We paid $1500 down for a brand new house—three bedrooms, two bathrooms and a big backyard. I was the crew, the planter, the painter—I made sixty yards of drapery. We made our own patio. I planted trees—I had blisters on my hands. I'd be up at four-thirty or five in the morning because if I wanted the woodwork to be a new color, I got up and painted it. I taught beginning Hebrew and made clothes for people.

If somebody was in trouble and needed money, we helped them raise money. One day, a friend who went through hell in the holocaust came to me crying. She and her husband had a little house and they were going to lose it. They were behind two months rent. I didn't have the money to help her. I told some ladies from the Temple that we needed to raise at least $150 for a couple who deserved help—no names mentioned. I provided all the food, and I don't remember what I charged in those days. maybe $5 or $8 per person because people didn't have a lot of money. I remember buying strawberries with long stems. I made blintzes, cakes, fruit and tuna and everyone had a wonderful time. We raised the money and they did not lose their house.

Sometimes, you cannot help somebody with money, but with a kind word or opening the right door or helping people even a little bit goes a long way. I want to say something nice that my husband did just last week. A couple that we reverted (David says converts are reverts) about 25 years ago were going to lose the house that they had rented for years because the landlord was going into foreclosure. They were going to be put out on the street. They needed $3,000 to move. We called our banker and asked if they could get a loan, but the banker said it could take up to a week. I said we needed the money by Monday—no later. They loaned us the money because they didn't know our friends. We wrote them the check and the bank cashed the check right then. If we get it back or not, God will help us—if not, we'll pay the bank off.

We know what it is to be hungry and not to have. Sometimes a kind word, help doing something nice—no matter whether they're Jewish or just a good person. If they stretch their hand out and ask for help, you cannot return their hand empty. Unfortunately, a lot of people are still bigoted, who are selfish and think, "If you don't look like me or go to my house of worship, I hate you." We see it every day.

Decorative Shalom plate.

Dear Mr. and Mrs. Kane,

I am so sorry to here about your family. If my mom had died I don't know what I would do. I don't know what I would do, I don't how I would eat. Thank you for teaching our class about the strugles of your young life.

Sincerely
Lamar

A million thank yous and I hope and wish that the rest of your lives are lived in peace and happiness.

Genesis Miranda

Throughout your speeches, tears were making their way out of my eyes, covering my eyelashes, and falling into my lap. Near the end while you were singing, the feeling in the gym was ascending up to the ceiling and off of our shoulders, just gliding through the air like a balloon a little girl just let go of to give to her family in heaven.

Brooke

Lakewood, CA 90713
May 14, 2010

Dear Mr. and Mrs. Kane,
    Thank you very much for coming out to our school to share your life experiences, especially to a teen age group that some times can get wild and loud. We manage to handle and control ourselves to listen to everything you both had to say and express to us. I enjoyed and admire every second you guys were there.
    I like how you, Mr. Kane, express your-self about Mrs. Kane I loved the way you introduced her to us it amazing the respect and honor ship you have towards her, I myself, was raised to treat every girl with respect no matter what. I loved the saying Mrs. Kane said, "Smile cause the every one will smile with you, but when you cry, you cry alone." That quote will stay with me forever it blow me away. I feel sorry about that picture and flashback you get Mr. Kane about your grand father. Hearing that brings me back to my very own grandfather when he passed away. You have an awesome voice. Mrs. Kane your a very strong woman and there's not that many of you out there stay strong and keep the faith. So as well to you Mr. Kane.

                        Sincerely,
                        Ivan Godinez

Olive Ave
CA 90805

Dear Mr. and Ms. Kane.

I could like to thank you for coming to our school and taking about your experiences with us. The way you both talked about the holocaust with smiles.well was very inspiring to everyone attending.And the songs you sang in the different languages made us go from sad to happy in a second.Your presence alone made the experience very exciting.

When you talked about the way how you had to sing for extra pieces of bread was extrodinary. The most amazing thing you said that day was when you and your wife talked about how you met and felt about each others experiences,is unwordable.It takes a lot of courage to tale about your experiences in the holocaust and to to do it so many times to different people of all ages.is special for the ones listening.I wish I could see the evil face of Hitler,if he was still alive to see that there was survivors of his camps that live well lives.some better than before.that would make all the survivors happy.

In all the experiences that you both talked about were one of the best experiences of my life and i hope that nothing like that ever happens again and I can I'll try to make sure that never happens.

Sincerly,

Francisco Martinez

I will express this to my future children that I met a holocaust survivor. Thank you, I will remember that day for the rest of my life.

Love,

Baldemar Garcia

I remember when you said that first people should fall in love, then get married and then have children and that it should not be the other way around. I like what you said and I will always remember that. It is memorable to me because in today's society it is hard to find people that think that way.

Sincerely,

Karla Tello

80

Dear Rabbi and Mrs. Kane,

I'm writing this letter to thank you for talking to my Peers and I. I am Jewish and have had close friends of the family go through the Holocaust. My G-d Mother Martha Posalski crossed the Alps into Italy, then moved a cross the country side to Viché France. She did this while being pregnant. Once she got to France, she helped the Resistence Movement.

Your visit to my School had a huge effect on me. I have read *Night* by Eliezer Wiesel, and *I will plant you a lilac tree* by Laura Hillman, whom I've heard talk seven times. Your stories are engraved in my heart, and I'll never forget you........ Never.

I've heard many Rabbi's say that the Sh'ma is the most important Prayer of all, but in my opinion the Kaddish is the most important in these dark times, with Israel on the brink of war with the Arabic Nations.

My father passed away on April 16, 2009, a few weeks ago, and it has been very hard. lately and I always think, why him? Why not the evil guys, why not the dictators, why not the people who only choose to hurt people? Why my father who was loving and whose only goal in life was to make everyone laugh and to help anyone for whatever reasons? But hearing your story helped me feel much better about the whole situation and it made me realize that it could have been worse. He died in a motorcycle accident, he collided with a truck. But you guys made me thankful that he didn't get beat or starved or anything that could have hurt him more because that would have been unbearable to me.

Thank you sincerely,

Veronica Quezada

No one has ever spoke to me in a way of having hope and truly wanting to survive after being through so much. It made me realize that compared to all my problems I haven't gone through anything and I just gave up on everything. But since the appreciated visit, it made me think about many things. Like the way both of you, Mr. and Mrs. Kane see everything around you as beautiful. From now on many things are going to change, physically but mostly mentally and emotionally.

Sincerely,

Yoly Quintero

Dear Mr. and Mrs. Kane,

Thank you for coming to Lakewood High and sharing your story with us. I'm truly sorry for your losses and what you guys went through. You are truly my inspiration. I'm glad you made it through. One thing that always going to stick on my mind because of Mrs. Kane is," If you smile, the world smiles with you, if you cry, you cry alone." I admire that advice. It shock me to hear Mrs. Kane speaks eight languages, that just proves to me anything is possible. You know, you are my favorite couple. I admire your relationship. Hopefully one day I'll have kids to share your story with. Once again Thank you and I wish you the best of the best for you and your kids.

Sincerly,
Jocelyn Murillo

Your visit was very meaningful
to me because I am Jewish and
I understood how you two felt
being discriminated against
because of your religion. I love
hearing stories from Jewish holocaust survivors because I feel like
I understand better than other
students. I think Jewish people
have the strongest connection
because of the holocaust. I
sometimes feel ashamed of my
religion because I got picked
on when I was a little kid. you
made me realize that there is
nothing to be ashamed of.

Leah Bloomfield

I would also like to add
that your faith in God
has truly touched me.

Lakewood, CA 90713
May 8, 2009

Dear Mr. and Mrs. Kane,

I am writing to thank you for your wonderful advice; it was very enlightening. Your words are inspiring. After listening to your stories, I began to think about how grateful I am for having what I have. It was truly an honor to have you both at our school that day.

Because of you two, my future seems brighter and my vision of it is broader. I have no limits to my dreams.

Your words will echo in my mind for years to come. It would be wonderful if you could come back some day. Thank you for inspiring us all.

Respectfully Yours,
Samantha Flores

Lakewood, CA 90713
May 8, 2009

Dear Mr. and Mrs. Kane,

Thank you for your speech yesterday. It was the best speech that I have ever heard. It was funny, and emotional at the same time. The Both of you made me think about how much life is in the United States. That education is every important because not everyone gets to learn.

Your speech was very meaningful because you made me change my mind about the way I treat people. I will respect more people and start to give to others. I also start to respect my friends and family and be glad that I can be with them everyday.

The only question I have is how did it feel when you were split up from your family? I love my family and if I lost them I don't know what I would do. Thank you for coming you have touch me hearts.

Sincerely,
Jeremy Didon.

You two are very kind and very inspiring people. I was amazed to see how calm and happy you two were, even though you have gone through hell. The thing that amazed me the most is the fact that both of you are not angry at the world for putting you what you went through. Mr. Kane was even making jokes! You are a funny guy. You have a nice voice, too.

Michael Madrid

I started thinking about how lucky I am to have an education, family, friends, food and especially freedom. I know that I take for granted the things that I have. Your speech made me realize that I should be very grateful for everything that I have.

Neida Medina

Few people in this world who have gone through terrible times and still had their faith in Him. I pray that God will give me the strength to have faith in Him during tough times just as you two had undying faith in Him. I am so grateful to have met you both. Your words have truly touched my heart and given me the determination to work harder and achieve my goals.

Everylastingly grateful,
Kassandra Duff

My grandfather also endured a few years in a concentration camp, but in the Vietnam War. Before he passed away in my childhood, he told me the true meaning of faith, love and trust. I thank you again for visiting us, and I should've asked for a hand-shake to tell my future family of my meeting with one of the successful and few holocaust survivors.

Steven Phong

I sincerely wish you both the best and that you become great grandparents.

Jessica Elderkin

Dear Rabbi and Mrs. Kane,
  Thank you very much for coming to my school. I learned a lot about the Holocaust. Like how the Jews had lines to see if they got gassed or not. I feel sorrow for the ones who were not so lucky because they could have had a better life. I can admit that I have said some things about Jewish people and I feel really bad about what I have said. It gave me a new perspective on what happened 65 yrs ago.
                    Sincerely,

                    Jordan Holland

I never understood how people could not be angry after something so terrible happens to them. You said that it was not God who did it, it was God's own children who were fighting and hating against each other. It helps me to believe that even when I have bad times, or something unexplainable happens, that if I have my faith in God, I will be okay.

Jyl Grotsky

Knowing that you never lost your faith in God has helped me to never lose faith.

Zachary Lee Witt

A million thank yous and I hope and wish that the rest of your lives are lived in peace and happiness.

Genesis Miranda

This is something I'm never going to forget and I'm sure my class-mates feel the same way. I don't know what it was, but when Mr. Kane went up there and started to sing, I felt something. I felt my heart full of joy and my skin shivered. I really can't explain my feeling. I just felt joy and love.

Sincerely,

David Perez

4-20-2009

Dear Rabbi & Mrs. Kane,
   I thank you for coming to our school, Marine View Middle School, and telling us of your experience. What you went though was a horrible nightmare. Your tears were strength; your words, eye openers. When I walked out I saw color. I saw the green leaves and grass, felt their softness and was glad. Glad that I live free, unjudged, and welcome. That night as I crawled into my warm, safe, bed I thanked God to have the life I have. Thanks to you I look at the world much differently, much more beautifully, than I did befor. Your Courage, strength and words will never leave me. Thank you again for talking to us.

Always,
Ashley Bentele

Milestones

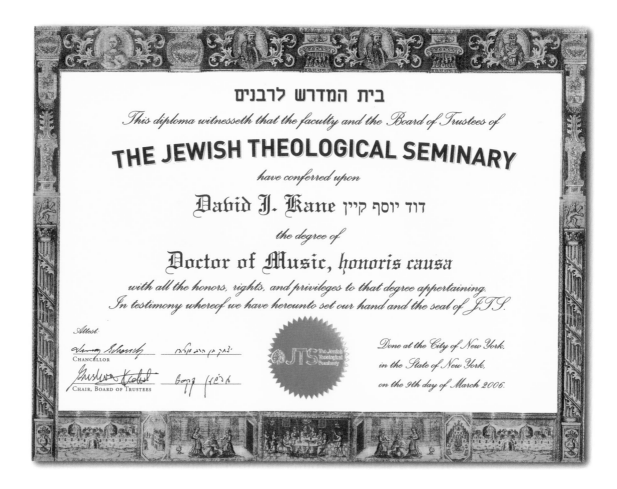

בית המדרש לרבנים

This diploma witnesseth that the faculty and the Board of Trustees of

THE JEWISH THEOLOGICAL SEMINARY

have conferred upon

David J. Kane דוד יוסף קיין

the degree of

Doctor of Music, honoris causa

with all the honors, rights, and privileges to that degree appertaining.
In testimony whereof we have hereunto set our hand and the seal of JTS.

Attest:

CHANCELLOR

CHAIR, BOARD OF TRUSTEES

Done at the City of New York,
in the State of New York,
on the 9th day of March 2006.

CANTORS ASSEMBLY
assembled on the occasion of its Sixty-Third Annual Convention
presents this prestigious

YUVAL AWARD
to

Hazzan David Kane

Rabbi-Hazzan David Kane is a precious link — from generation to generation among cantors and the Jewish people, and between contemporary American Jewish life and the rich bygone life of European Jewry. Born in Poland, he spent some of the precious years of his youth in concentration camps, but was liberated from Buchenwald in 1945.

He began a new life in the United States in 1949 upon his arrival in Los Angeles. This included further secular and religious education, leading to a successful career as a spiritual leader in a number of California congregations, especially Temple Beth Shalom of Long Beach, where he served for over 25 years prior to being recognized as Hazzan-emeritus. He has been twice recognized with Honorary Doctorate degrees — in California and by the Jewish Theological Seminary.

Deeply dedicated to his wife of 58 years, Yetta, and his children, grandchildren and great-grandchild, he has also been tremendously loyal to his colleagues in the cantorate, and has been a significant leader in and extremely generous to the Cantors Assembly.

His life, his energy, his accomplishments serve as an unending source of pride and inspiration to his colleagues.

May the Almighty grant Hazzan Kane many years of good health and joy in a world at peace.

May 5, 2010 – 21 Iyar 5770

PRESIDENT	EXECUTIVE VICE PRESIDENT	EXECUTIVE ADMINISTRATOR

The Long Beach Hebrew Academy

Under the Auspices of the
Central Organization for Jewish Education — Lubavitch

3981 ATLANTIC AVENUE, LONG BEACH, CALIFORNIA 90807

RABBI EPHRAIM PIEKARSKI
Founder Co-Director
RABBI GERSHON SCHUSTERMAN
Co-Director
RABBI MOSHE Y. ENGEL
Director Religious Education

November 27, 1972

TELEPHONES
424-9787
426-2687
774-3747

To whom it may concern:

This is to ascertain that there came before me Rabbi David Kane whom I have known for the past three years as a man of praiseworthy character and qualifications.

Rabbi Kane showed me a certificate of ordination issued by Rabbi Singer of Los Angeles, on July 29, 1957.

After examining this certificate of ordination I can testify that it states unequivocally that Rabbi David Kane is an ordained Rabbi and that he can perform all Rabbinical functions.

Respectfully

Rabbi Ephraim Piekarski

REP/jf

UNITED SYNAGOGUE OF AMERICA

6525 Sunset Boulevard • Los Angeles, California 90028 • HOllywood 3-1161

TRANSLATION OF LETTER OF ORDINATION ISSUED TO
RABBI DAVID KANE FROM RABBI ITZHAK MEIR KORMAN

        Rabbi Itzhak Meir Korman
        Settlement of Zichron Moshe
        20 Chofetz Chaim Street
        Jerusalem

With the help of God, the month of Av in the year
of 5724, in the Holy City of Jerusalem.

This is to certify that Rabbi David Joseph, son
of Yaakov Koppel Kane, who was born in the
country of Poland in Europe, in the year 5688,
a refugee of the holocaust, who studied in the
Yeshivot of the Diaspora in Europe, is known
as a scholar, an ordained rabbi, who is God-fearing
and pleasant in his relations with others.

The abovenamed is capable of serving as a Rabbi
and spiritual leader in one of the Jewish communities
of the Diaspora.

        With the blessing of our Holy Torah
        and those who study it,

        Signed: Yitzhak Meir Korman
(followed by the official seal, which appears in
Hebrew and its own translation)

This is to certify that the above is an accurate
translation of the Hebrew document which, as
indicated, has been translated by me.

        Rabbi Edward M. Tenenbaum

CERTIFICATE of ORDINATION

Be it known that I the undersigned
am honored and privileged to declare that

Rabbi DAVID JAY KANE

as studied under my jurisdiction all religious codes in regard to Kashrut of both
dairy and meat products. Be it also
known that he has satisfactorily completed all required studies of the hebrew
civil code; and has shown his extensive
knowledge in Torah, Talmudic learning and
Rabbinic lore; I therefore ordain him as Rabbi
& highly recommend him to any orthodox
community as spiritual leader whose qualifications are praiseworthy.

Given this 29th day of July 1957.

Singer

Examined by me
on May 18, 1965

Edward M Tenenbaum,
Rabbi

תעוֹדת סמיכה

אוכל להודיע בשער בת רבים שהרב ר'

דוד יוסף הכהן שליט"א
בר יעקב קופל הי"ו.

למד אצלי ביורה דעה וחלק ראשון הלכות
שחיטה וטרפות ומליחה בשר וחלב בתערובת
וגם כן אורח חיים הלכות שבת ובאבן העזר
הלכות קדושין וידיו רב לו בהלכות העלוי
וכל מין דין סמיכא לנו יורה יורה והקהלה
אשר תבחר בו ימצא נוזת כמלבד שהוא
תלמוד וחכם גדול ובעל מידות תרומיות
וירא שמים באמת ותמים.
ועל זה באתי על החתום
ב' דר"ח מנחם אב שנת תשי"ז לפ"ק
לאס אנדזשעלעס, קליפורניא.

Dr. Rabbi
Menach Singer
Los Angeles

96

Silver Purim Megilla, a gift from Rabbi Bernard Kimmel, acquired in Cochin, India where there is a large Jewish community.

Moses on Mount Sinai receiving the Ten Commandments. David says, "This was the beginning of our faith." The sterling figurine was acquired in Bethlehem. Yetta remembers, "An armed Israeli who spoke Arabic took us in a Mercedes to a souk, an open-air marketplace, where we found this treasure."

50th Wedding Anniversary cruise to the Mexican Riviera. From top to bottom: Jerry, Berry, Teri, Michael, Jerry Kaufman, Bryna, Alex, Emily, Elisa, David Z, Hilary (Minnie's granddaughter), Minnie Kaplan, David, Yetta, Malah and Sam Langholz, Charlie.

L'Dor Vador

From generation to generation

Kane
Family
Tree

David Kane's Family

Gedalye Nudelman was a shoemaker.

Pearl Nudelman was a midwife.

Gedalye Nudelman
(grandfather)
Pearl Nudelman
(grandmother)

Menachem Mendel Koplowicz
(grandfather)
Reizel Koplowicz
(grandmother)

Brajndla (Nudelman) Koplowicz
(mother)

Kople (Karol) Koplowicz
(father)

Pearl Koplowicz
(sister, nickname: Polesia)

DAVID KANE
(Born: Dawid Josef Koplowicz)

Berry Kane
(son)
Teri (Ravel) Kane
(daughter-in-law)

Bryna (Kan
(daughter)
Jerrold (Jerr
(son-in-law

Emily Kane
(granddaughter)

Alex Kane
(grandson)
Lindsay (Lassen) Kane
(granddaughter-in-law)

Charlie Kane
(grandson)

Michael Kaufman
(grandson)

Yetta Kane's Family

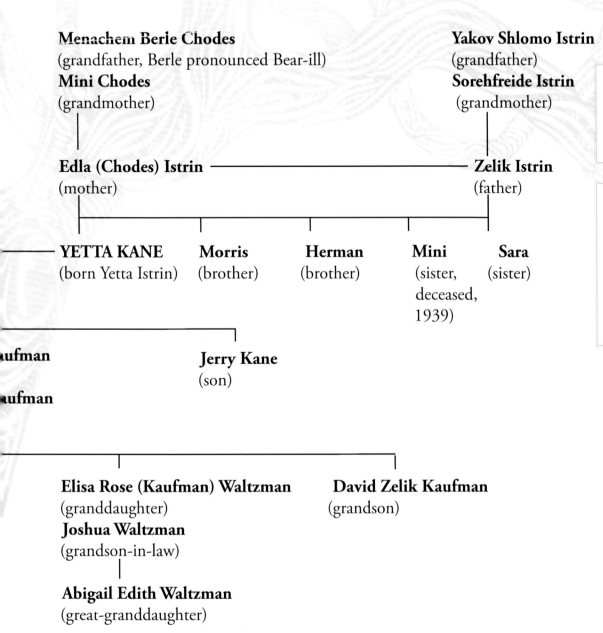

Menachem Berle Chodes
(grandfather, Berle pronounced Bear-ill)
Mini Chodes
(grandmother)

Yakov Shlomo Istrin
(grandfather)
Sorehfreide Istrin
(grandmother)

Edla (Chodes) Istrin ———————————— **Zelik Istrin**
(mother)   (father)

YETTA KANE   **Morris**   **Herman**   **Mini**   **Sara**
(born Yetta Istrin)   (brother)   (brother)   (sister,   (sister)
                                                          deceased,
                                                          1939)

aufman   **Jerry Kane**
                (son)

aufman

Elisa Rose (Kaufman) Waltzman   **David Zelik Kaufman**
(granddaughter)   (grandson)
Joshua Waltzman
(grandson-in-law)

Abigail Edith Waltzman
(great-granddaughter)

Menachem Berle was
tall and handsome.
He was a butcher.

Mini Chodes passed
away when her
daughter, Edla,
was just 5 years
old. Morris Istrin is
named for her.

David and Yetta at Ike Langholz' wedding. Here, Yetta is pregnant with Bryna.

Chapter Five
Our dear children: Bryna, Berry & Jerry

BRYNA

Yetta

When Bryna was born on February 2, 1955, it was a very, very special moment, and especially since we wanted a little girl so badly to name after Brajndla, may she rest in peace. Bryna was a beautiful, beautiful child from the day she was born. She looked like Daddy—she had a peachy complexion, beautiful skin and no hair. She was very loving, very sweet—always such a special gift to us. Today she is a doctor, a dermatologist with a busy practice. We are so proud of Bryna.

Bryna never said no to anything we asked her to do and was good at playing the piano, did beautiful sculpture work and studied hard. She always wanted to do the right thing and she always wanted to please her parents. She was on the quiet side and very modest. The kids in school used to call her a "nerd," because she always studied and never went any place. Her friends felt we were sometimes overprotective and wouldn't let her go places that most girls went in those days. We suggested that when she grew up and was on her own, she could then make the choices and would be old enough to judge. Those were the rules in our home and she was always very obedient. Always a good student and willing to do the very, very best. It was very pleasant and beautiful to see her reach maturity when she finished high school with high honors and was accepted to UCLA. Before she went to UCLA, she volunteered hundreds of hours as an interpreter for teachers.

Zelik and Edla at their home on Laurel Avenue, Los Angeles.

She spoke fluent Spanish and was always good in languages. She was called a *Candy Stripe Girl*. Some of those teachers and professors are some of her best friends today.

We would take the kids in the car sightseeing, with their grandparents, Edla and Zelik. Bubbe and Zeyda were so kosher—more kosher than most rabbis, maybe. Edla had a dish towel for meat and one for dairy. The dish towel used for dairy was not to be hung next to the meat towel. That's how strict she was. We were going to Palm Springs one day and Bryna was about five or six, it was before Jerry was born. We stopped and decided to go into a restaurant and get a cup of coffee. Bryna was walking with Edla, bless her memory, and as we opened the door, she smelled a strong smell of bacon and Bryna threw up right in the doorway. We apologized to Edla and she said, "It serves you right to go to a *treyf* restaurant with the children." We nearly died of embarrassment right on the spot. (Chuckles)

David

Bryna always was inquisitive. She married Jerry Kaufman, a fine, upstanding man, and she is a devoted mother to Michael, Elisa and David. Today, she participates in a charitable program called "Erase the Past" for gang members. That came about from meeting our friends who were survivors and had numbers on their hands that were tattooed by the Germans. Neither of us were tattooed during the war, luckily. Anyway, Bryna was very, very inquisitive about why they wanted to hide their numbers and what it was all about. She said that one day she was going to do something to erase their past. Every gang member that she gives an hour to gives five hours of community service back. She became very famous for this program. She paid for the beginning of that program and made us very proud. She is the founding partner and co-owner of the Laser Skin Care Center Dermatology Associates in Long Beach. She has clinical teaching appointments at UCLA and UC Irvine where she's Assistant Clinical Professor of Medicine/Dermatology. Bryna wants to help people and still does—every day of her life.

BERRY

Yetta

When we were blessed to have another child, it didn't matter whether it was a boy or girl, being that we had a beautiful daughter already. Bryna was 14 months old, to the day, when Berry was born on April 2, 1956. I went to the same hospital, with the same nurses and doctor and even the same bed. They said, "You're here again?" We had this darling boy, who weighed 8 pounds, 13 ounces, and 21 inches long. I decided to name him Menachem Berle which translates as Maurice Berry but my husband didn't like the name, so it was changed. Berry was very sweet—very loving. We had no problems, with any of our children, God bless them, they were very healthy and happy children. They grew up beautifully together. Bryna was like a little mommy to Berry, and was very helpful. Today, Berry is a corporate attorney in San Jose, an accomplished professional and devoted family man. We are so delighted with our Berry.

One day, when Berry was about four years old, we had a '56 Oldsmobile and the car was parked in the driveway. We lived on a hill and I went back in the house for something. Bryna got out of the car just as Berry climbed in front and released either the brake or put the car in gear, and the car started to roll back. Bryna ran in the house yelling that Berry was driving the car. Meanwhile, a neighbor chased the car down the hill and stopped it.

The first five years we frequently spoke in Yiddish – the Jewish language— especially when we didn't want the children to hear what we were saying.

Friends told us unless we started speaking English all the time, we would have a hard time. So, we switched to English rain or shine. The children started to go to a special Jewish day school, the Breed Street Shul in Boyle Heights.

Berry was a very bright child, and very different from Bryna. He was "all boy" and he loved to play with little soldiers. Berry, even though he is blessed with a sharp mind, we had to remind him to study and push him a little bit. He believed in playing and having fun more than studying. He still had very, very good grades.

David

Berry was always determined and he could have been a master sergeant because when Berry says something—it's his way or the highway. He turned into a great cook. Berry is what we call a mensch—he is as honest as the day is long and would not partake in any questionable dealings. We think if he was elected the Attorney General of California, the state would have a very good man in that office.

He's a very protective person. When he was going on the bus with Bryna to the Jewish day school, somebody started to bother Bryna and Berry didn't like it. A fight started and Berry took a lunch pail over the head. In

Happy times at Edla and Zelik's house. Left to right: David, Bryna, Edla, Berry, Zelik, Olie, Sara, Joe, Morris and Leslie (Morris' late wife, blessed memory). 1958–59

109

retaliation, Berry flattened the other boy's head on the closed window of the bus. Berry needed stitches after that.

Berry had a classmate named Seth Stern, and they went camping overnight in the mountains. They were about 17 years old. They set up their tent for the night and settled down. Meanwhile, at home, we were lying in bed, well past midnight, and I said to Yetta, "I hope our Berenue is having a good time, and a bear won't hurt him." Yetta said to me, "Go to sleep, go to sleep," and ignored me.

Meanwhile, back at the tent, it was a cold and rainy night, and all of a sudden something started pulling on the tent from outside. It was a mother brown bear and her cub and the boys could see her breath coming through the tent. Berry had to keep Seth from jumping out of his skin.

About four in the morning, the doorbell rang. Berry had his own key to the house, so we couldn't understand why the doorbell was ringing. He came in and said bears tried to invade their tent, and they had to scare them off with flashlights and rocks. It was very funny, but very frightening.

Berry also has two wonderful friends, Tom Miller and Carl Sternberg. They feel like part of our family and come to all the bar and bat mitzvahs and weddings. When they were all going to high school. I did something some fathers wouldn't do. The boys wanted to drink and I said, "If you want to drink, it's right here in the house, potato chips and beer." We didn't want them to get into trouble outside the home and this way they could learn to have a responsible drink at home. We all played cards together. I joined them wearing boxer shorts, a wife-beater t-shirt, dark socks, furry slippers and lots of gold chains and rings. We had a great time.

Tom Miller is now the Chief Medical Officer at the University of Utah

Hospital in Salt Lake. Carl is an internal technology consultant to large corporations. They are all doing very well—all reached their goals.

Berry went to school and graduated UCLA as a history major, and then went to McGeorge School of Law. He said if he didn't pass the bar the first time, he was not going to try again. We told him that he would pass it the first time and he did.

Yetta was still working when Berry married his love, Teri, a talented landscape architect, and they lived in Davis for two years until Emily was born. Then they settled in San Jose where Alex and Charlie arrived.

One time they were going out of town to a wedding and Yetta went to stay with the grandkids. She took two bags of frozen salad, frozen chicken and things you couldn't get there at the store because there weren't that many kosher places in San Jose. She was running to catch the plane, all dressed up, and one of the bags tore and the whole chicken was on the floor. A man said, "Ma'am, ain't they got any chickens where you's going?"

Today, Berry is a successful corporate attorney with SanDisc, a high-tech company in Silicon Valley. He has a wonderful family and we love him and are very, very proud of him.

JERRY

Yetta

In 1964 we took our first real vacation, a trip to Israel. We came back pregnant with Jerry. He was blessed to be born April 7, 1965, about ten years after Bryna and Berry, when we were better off. Jerry cemented the family back together as the third child in the family.

David

On my 80th birthday, in front of about 70 guests in our home, Jerry gave the most beautiful speech. He always had a magnificent speaking voice and competed in public speaking as a child. Even today, he could be a top radio personality if he chose to be. I will never forget the heartfelt things he said on my birthday.

Yetta

Jerry was a brave little boy, even as a baby. We caught him one time, standing on top of the crib, just before he was about to jump off. Of course it was good he was brave, because when he got older, Berry used to put sheets on, and pretend he was a ghost, just to scare his little brother. Today Jerry is a real estate professional and very active with computers. He is a tremendous help to us, very caring and attentive. We adore our Jerry.

Jerry was always loving and honest but he had to learn a lesson early on.

He was just three years old and he had some gum in his pocket. We asked, "Where did you get it?" He said, "From the store." We said, "So how much did you pay?" He said, "I didn't pay, I just took it." We said, "In that case we're going back to the store and you're going to apologize to the man." We told him that they put people in jail for doing things like that. He was crying big, crocodile tears. He apologized and promised that he would never do anything like that again.

When Jerry was six or seven, one of his teachers told us he was a genius. They called him Little Einstein. He had a very kind heart and is very smart. He also had a few seizures as a boy, that affected his motor coordination, but he grew out of it. Jerry was active in the Boy Scouts and American Zion Association.

David

One day when we were not home, some people came to the door looking for food. Jerry didn't have any money to give them, so he took a chicken out of the freezer and gave it to them. If someone asked him for money, he would tell them to come with him and he would buy them something to eat. A couple of times he found money in a store and brought it to the counter and they took his name. When nobody claimed the money, the store called him and he got to keep it. One time he got $8 and another time $10.

Jerry attended the Long Beach State College and Orange Coast University, and studied for almost seven years. He has a lot of knowledge and we are blessed to have him. He lives close by, is very loving, very attentive and very kind. He is good-natured and we hope someday that he finds his *beshert* (his meant-to-be) and gets married. But, marriage is not for everyone and if he doesn't want to get married, it's fine.

He acquired a good business sense and has an acumen for real estate and computers. He's a good conversationalist, and a glib tongue when it comes to politics, sports and historical events. We love him. And that's what life is all about.

We have three children and each one is a diamond. Each one, to us, is equally dear, and we don't care what the situation is. We have truly been blessed with three wonderful children.

The dark-colored shofar was acquired by Rabbi Bernard Kimmel in Cochin, India. It is over 100 years old. The light-colored shofar is from Israel. Both are from David's collection.

FAMILY VACATIONS

The best times we had in our lives was with family. We took little vacations, as we could afford them. The first 15 years of our marriage, we didn't go very far—San Diego, Las Vegas and Palm Springs. We always took Edla and Zelik. We didn't have a lot of money, but they would always come with two bags on the bus: salami, hot dogs, bobkeh and chocolate. Things we couldn't get around Monterey Park in the grocery store around the corner. They would bring herring and pickles.

We went to San Diego—Shelter Island—and drove "Betsy," an old Chevy station wagon—an old battle-ax, really beaten up. When we went to Vegas almost 50 years ago, Yetta drove and she used to make it in four and a half hours while everybody slept. We used to stay at the Sahara where they had a babysitting service—you could leave the kids and go to watch a show, as they slept. When we were done watching the show, we picked the kids up. We got to know quite a few people and made quite a few trips to Vegas. We didn't go to gamble. Yetta wouldn't put in a wooden nickel to this day. David's adopted brother, Joe Kohn, was the cantor at one of the big synagogues, Beth Shalom. He knew people from the Sands and other hotels, so we would go to shows and have a good time.

We got to know Sammy Davis, Jr. and Frank Sinatra. They were big shots and used to gamble a lot. We knew Myron Cohen and would get front seats at his show. Don Rickles and all the other comedians—Shelley Winters, Steve Lawrence and Eydie Gorme. A lot of the old timers. We used to get a lot of comps, but we would pay sometimes too. We met hotel owners, like Jack Entratter and Nat King Cole. We met Nat King Cole at the Sands. At the time, it was the big hotel for all the people that were coming up in show business. Mr. Entratter was the president of the Temple Beth Sholom, and the owner of the hotel, and a very fine gentleman. He would get us kosher steaks when we stayed there. We met Jackie Mason and Jerry Lewis and Dean Martin. You could stand and watch them gamble, and the money was rolling. The Sands was the oldest, biggest and fanciest, and was the hotel where all the entertainers got their big start. Mr. Entratter was a tremendous business man and would book only the top entertainers. The hotel was always filled to the brim.

Sammy Davis, Jr. was funny. He adopted the Jewish faith— converted to Judaism. Rabbi Max Nussbaum, from Temple Israel of Hollywood, was his mentor and converted him. He was a Reform rabbi. He said, "So how will I know where you will be sitting in the temple, Sammy?" Sammy said, "I'll be the only guy wearing a white yarmulke." One night, Sammy got up and sang one of the Kol Nidres.

We would go to Palm Springs with Edla and Zelik. They would get in the backseat of the car—Bubbe and Zeyde and the children, with a big ten-pound salami and a *fleysh*-knife for cutting meat. Tomatoes and cucumbers were peeled in the car with a loaf of rye or pumpernickel bread, and a big bottle of Coca-Cola. Why would you peel cucumbers in the car? Because if you peeled them before, they wouldn't be as fresh. When you freshly peel them, the flavor is there. After you peel them and wrap them up, they don't taste the same. And tomatoes are delicious right when you cut them. If you cut them ahead, it's not the same flavor. So, all those things were done in the backseat of the car with a big, white towel on their lap. It was a tradition that came with them from Europe.

The kids liked chocolate, so Edla would buy the "parve," non-dairy chocolate. A huge one, like a pound. She'd break off a big chunk, a quarter of a pound and say, "Here, kid, have a piece." They would bring halvah and a bopkeh, which is challah, but with lots more sugar and shortening. Roll it out, add cocoa, lots of chocolate chips, roll it up, and make it into a big bun. Put sugar and nuts on top and break off a piece. No knife was needed because it was soft. Or you could add cinnamon, raisins and nuts—almost like a bundt cake. And that was for the road when we took our family on vacations.

When our family grew up, we went to Hawaii with the Kaufmans, as well as Maui. We celebrated Elisa's Sweet 16 birthday at the Ritz Carlton. A family reunion in Israel was joyous with our Israeli relatives.

OUR BELOVED PARENTS
Edla, Zelik, Kople & Brajndla

Yetta

My mother, Edla, was always smiling and always content with her lot in life and she always said that if you look too high, you'll never be satisfied; if you look a little bit lower you'll see how blessed you are. Look at yourself and count the blessings that you have, see how many people are less fortunate.

Zelik and Edla at their home on Laurel Avenue, Los Angeles. 1965–70

She was very, very religious, but still modern. When somebody was in the hospital, she would clean their house, get money together to buy groceries so that when they came back from the hospital, there was food in the refrigerator and the house was clean. Not too many people do that. The most religious rabbis from Israel would always stop at our home, and Mom always gave a lot of charity. My parents felt, and we feel the same, that the more you give, the more Hashem blesses you and gives back so much more. It's true.

My father was very, very hard working in the junk business—buying old cars, metals and junk, which he resold.

David

If my father-in-law, Zelik, promised some charity, the next day it was paid. He also was mindful of doing the right thing. He was a very strong man—physically and mentally. He was very good at math and was a very good businessman. He, unfortunately, passed away in 1971 from prostate cancer.

Once there was a woman on the street and a young thug tried to steal her purse and Zelik took off after him. People used to come around to his junkyard and steal hubcaps, so Zelik made the decision that he was going to sleep all night, with a stick, under the desk in the office. He had no gun, no nothing. And so he slept under the desk and two teenagers came to steal and he got out from under the desk and grabbed both of them with one hand and called the police. He was so strong—so strong.

Zelik at his home on Laurel Avenue, Los Angeles.

My father, Kople, was 46 years old in 1949 and a relatively young man. He invested in the stock market and made quite a bit of money. He saved every penny and wouldn't spend very much. He bought a Smith-Corona typewriter and made sure that I learned how to type. I had to type in the bathroom because the people who lived below us didn't like the noise. I would put the typewriter on the sink.

Kople remarried, to a lady by the name of Helen Goldberg Shuman. They met in Germany but married here. It really didn't work out. They were divorced a short time before she passed away. As I told you, some of the people came out of the concentration camps physically okay but mentally

scarred. I bought him for his birthday, many times, shirts and ties. When he passed away, I found them in his closet—never worn. He was very proud of our children, but didn't appreciate Yetta as much, in the beginning, because he felt that I was the cat's meow and should marry a princess. I did marry a princess, but he didn't realize it. As time went on, my father grew to love Yetta.

I wish that he would have lived more and spent more on himself, and not worried about leaving what he did to us. He liked jokes and thought he was a comedian and I inherited that from him. He passed away at the age of 82 and I am right now wearing the watch that he wore, a Bulova. Yetta took it to a jeweller to have it refurbished. I have two very beautiful, expensive watches, but I prefer to wear this one.

Kople liked Henny Youngman, especially the line, "Take my wife, please." In his sixties, he took on the habit of not trusting people. He became like a fellow from Missouri, the "show me" state. You had to show him things in order for him to believe it.

Yetta once got a call from his wife Helen, may she rest in peace, who said, "Daddy's in the hospital and he had a heart attack and is dying." We ran down to Kaiser Hospital, Emergency, and there was my father, who was supposedly deathly sick and dying, sitting up, eating a tuna sandwich.

When I bought my first Cadillac—a used 1965 Cadillac—his expression was, "Oh, big shot, something better you couldn't buy?"

He loved Bryna and Emily. He said, "Emily is going to be a Venus." He was right, of course. He was proud of everything I did. May he rest in peace and may he know peace where he is and be reunited with my mother, Brajndla, bless her memory, who was very good to him and was an outstanding, educated woman. It was her wisdom that saved both our lives on the day of liberation in Buchenwald concentration camp. My father had learned from her that sick people should not eat heavy food. When our liberators served a rich, beef stew when we were still very sick, Kople warned me not to eat it. He knew from watching my mother work and listening to her. So even though Brajndla, and my sister Pearl, had already been murdered by the Nazis, before liberation day, and although many others died on liberation because their bodies could not handle the heavy food, my mother's wisdom saved us.

It also strikes me, that when I saw my daughter Bryna, at my 80th birthday party, talking to my five-month old great-granddaughter, that she reminds me of my blessed mother Branjdla. "Hello Abigail, Bubbe loves you. I love you so much Abigail." The same spirit, the same enormous love for children is in Bryna. She inherited this, body and soul from Branjdla, whom she is named after.

Bubbe and Zeyde enjoy time with Abigail Edith.

50th Wedding Anniversary cruise. Left to Right: Elisa, Jerry Kaufman, Michael, Yetta, David, Bryna, David Z.

OUR PRECIOUS GRANDCHILDREN

MICHAEL

Michael lives in Tel Aviv, Israel, continuing his successful career in television. He has producer credits on at least twenty different shows from MSNBC to Bravo to Showtime and he knows all aspects of production. He's a world traveler and studied in Italy on a Guggenheim Fellowship. His MFA in Film Producing and Writing is from Columbia University.

Yetta

When Michael and his father Jerry Kaufman came to our lives, Michael was sweet, kind, loving and adorable. The first time I met him he came with a little suitcase, in little pajamas and a bathrobe to our home on Elm Avenue. Bryna and Jerry were going to have a date and Michael didn't have a babysitter, so Bubbe and Zeyde stepped forward. Elisa was almost three, and so excited that Michael was going to come over and sleep until Mom and Dad came home from the date.

We watched Michael grow up to become a sweet, pleasant, handsome young man—a special grandson with blue eyes. Mike would always wink and say, "I look just like Bubbe and I'm fair-complected like Bubbe." I would wink back and say,"That's right Michael, because you're Bubbe's boy."

David

Michael is a wonderful grandson. We are sorry he lives so far away, but it's very special and meaningful that he is in Israel. He is doing wonderful things with his life.

I look at all the things he's worked on, all the television projects, and all his international studies, and it's a wonder he fit so much into his young life. He also has an interest in teaching and curating. Like his parents and grandparents, Michael is a member of the Jewish National Fund, caretakers of the land of Israel for over a century. In New York City, Michael served on the board of "JNF Future." He's a go-getter is our Michael, and we know we don't have to wish him success, because he has a bushel of it already, but we will anyway. We love you, Michael.

Congratulations to Michael and his partner Juan Ortin, who married in 2011 in Buenos Aires.

ELISA ROSE

Elisa was ordained in 2009 by the Academy for Jewish Religion in Los Angeles, where she received a Masters Degree in Jewish Sacred Music. Prior to becoming a Cantor, she earned both her Masters and Bachelors Degrees in music and opera from the University of Southern California Thornton School of Music.

Yetta

When we went to the hospital when Elisa was born, she looked like a little china doll. We were, in a way, her surrogate parents because Mommy was interning and she had to be at the hospital for many hours at a time.

The first year of her birth, I was there every morning to give her a bath. The only time I didn't bathe her was when her Mommy was at home. She stayed with us—we took her places, she slept with us and of all our grandchildren, we spent the most time with her.

David

Elisa Rose, I am so proud of her and her accomplishments. She is a superb vocalist. No grandfather could be any prouder. I feel that eventually, if she keeps progressing the way she does, that she will be one of the finest cantors, God willing, anywhere in the world.

Elisa married Joshua Waltzman. Joshua is very, very accomplished and plays a variety of instruments including the piano and clarinet. He studied business, graduated medical school and got an MD/MBA, which is rare. He was chosen by the University of Rochester (New York) to enter the Plastic Surgery Program.

The greatest thing that happened to Yetta and I in our lifetime together was when we became great-grandparents because Josh and Elisa gave us our great-granddaughter, Abigail Edith. Abigail is a gift not just to us, but to everyone in our family, and especially to all our children and grandchildren. L'Dor Vador. From one generation to another, as it is said in Hebrew.

DAVID ZELIK

David will graduate from the University of California, Santa Barbara in 2012. At the College of Creative Studies he majors in neurobiology with a minor in Spanish and Spanish composition. He's devoted himself to volunteer work in the sciences, he played with the Long Beach Poly Symphony Orchestra for four years, and he's a competitive tennis player. He is also an accomplished Torah reader, an art that is mastered by very few people and even fewer young people.

Yetta

David Zelik is a sweetheart and we love him. There was not a day that we didn't see him when he was at home. He always liked to ride his scooter, play with the dogs—he loved animals.

One time when he was about five years old, it was raining, and a little girl who had a visual impairment was crying because her shoes got wet. She was very upset. David Zelik walked over, took her by the hand, and said, "Look, I'm going to take off my shoes too. See? I don't mind being barefoot. It's not cold, so you stop crying." He took her by the hand and took her around to where she was supposed to be. From that time, I could see David's beautiful soul. I'm happy to say he hasn't changed a bit, and it's been a pleasure to watch him grow up into a handsome young man.

When he was little, and very active, Zeyde didn't want to lose him when we went out. So I said, "You go next to Zeyde, and hold Zeyde's hand. I don't want Zeyde to get lost." He held on nice and tight, and he never lost his Zeyde.

David

David Zelik came along and cemented the unity of the Kaufman family. He was the "gift child," a very, very smart, young man.

We visited him at the university and got to see a little bit of his life there. He wrote a paper on his laboratory studies and decided that he is going into medicine.

David Z. has a beautiful voice and plays the cello. As a matter of fact, he told my daughter, "Mommy, I think I was born in the wrong generation." He loves Frank Sinatra. He knows where he comes from and where he wants to go. I feel that he is carrying out the wishes of my daughter and her husband and he is going in the right direction.

David is named after my son-in-law's father, whose name was David and also for Yetta's father, blessed memory, Zelik. So, he is named after two wonderful people and to this day, everyone calls him David Z.

EMILY

Emily completed her degree at the University of Arizona James E. Rogers College of Law in Tucson. She won the Dannie Lee Chandler Award for making a special contribution to the advancement of First Amendment values. Before that, she studied at the University of California, Los Angeles.

Emily is a world traveler; she studied in Spain and worked in Thailand for the Global Justice Center. Currently, she works for ROLL Global, a privately held US corporation.

David

Emily is our grandchild who, if she could fix the world and repair it, and everybody in it would be happy, that would be perfect for her. She is very smart and sweet. We are very proud of her and her accomplishments because she followed in her father's footsteps and passed the California State Bar to become an attorney.

Yetta

I used to fly up to San Jose when Emily was growing up, and would give her baths, sing songs, and play with her. I taught her how to make matzo ball soup. I taught her the love of Yiddishkeit. She would always say, "Bubbe, tell me stories about Europe, about when you were growing up." We would make hamentashen together for Purim; we would make potato pancakes and crepes together. When we made hamenstashen, she would have flour all over her nose, saying, "Bubbe, if I pinch the hamentashen, will it stay together?" She is very much like my dear mother, Edla.

She wanted to learn how to sew, so I got her a sewing machine. It was so much fun and she was always smiling and happy. It has been so much fun to see her grow up into the beautiful young lady she is. If I say to her mother that she shouldn't be doing something like driving a long way alone, Bryna says, "Mom, what do you want? She's like you. Don't blame us."

She's very giving and has a good heart and loves her siblings and cousins.

My brother's grandchildren call Emily "Little Bubbe Yetta." She would fly up from L.A. to Arizona to make a Shabbat meal for them. She would see that she gathered my brother's grandchildren, and her brother and Lindsay, and take them all to Shul and do things for the holidays. This is my Emily—no wonder they call her Bubbe Yetta.

ALEX

Alex has a Bachelor of Fine Arts from the University of Arizona in Visual Communications. He is working in the field of advertising now, a field many felt he was destined for. His creative vision is unique and has quickly been noticed in a competitive world.

David

Alex was always on the go and never needed a minute's rest. As a boy, he was like quicksilver. He has grown to be a sophisticated husband and successful commercial artist.

He met his wife, Lindsay Lassen, at the University of Arizona. Lindsay is from New Orleans and a very beautiful and talented young lady. She is another joy given to us by God.

Alex loves to cook and takes after his father in his love for cooking and being a great husband. He's an avid water-polo player. He's also a very creative guy and a real "people person."

Yetta

Alex is a sweetheart and looks a great deal like my grandfather— Zeyde Menachem Berle (pronounced Bear-ill). He is tall and handsome and has blue, hazel-grey eyes and light hair. When he was little, he had blonde

50th Wedding Anniversary cruise. From left to right: Emily, Charlie, Teri, Berry, Yetta, David, and Alex.

curls. He was very sweet and when I bathed him, he would say, "Bubbe, no soap. No soap." He would cry if soap got into his eyes. So I would lay him down in the bathtub and I would tell him, "Look up at the sky and look at the little butterflies on the ceiling and no soap will get in your eyes." He would say, "Bubbe, will you tell me a story?" Or he would say, "Bubbe, give me a body press." A body press was when they would lay down flat on the floor and I would pretend to run and run, and fall on top of them and make a pletzel (a flat Jewish cracker) out of them.

In the morning, in bed, Alex would say, "Bubbe, five more minutes, please, just five more minutes." To wake him up, I would ask him what he wanted for dinner that night, and he would tell me matzo balls and chicken soup. To this day, he could live on matzo balls and chicken soup. I would say, "Alex, you already had two bowls and you want more?" When he got bigger, he would help me make matzo balls and we would bake challah for Shabbat and the flour would be all over the counter. We love him deeply and it is just great to be around him.

CHARLIE

Charlie is earning his degree from the University of California Berkeley with a major in history and a minor in film studies, focusing on screenwriting. He expects to graduate in May, 2012. He interned with CBS television in the writers' office for the remake of Melrose Place.

Yetta

Charles Kane is very unique, kind and loving, and loves fitness and sports. He loves to eat well but he stays thin through exercise, and taking care of himself. He was in water polo, like his brother.

When he was growing up, I had a hard time getting him out of bed to go to school. I used to have to jump on top of him and tickle his toes and make him laugh. I would tell him that if he didn't get up, I wasn't going to make any more matzo balls for him. He was always very loving and never got angry with me, but he tried to pull the covers over his head so I wouldn't bother him. I would tell him that he had five minutes to eat breakfast and he would tell me he wasn't hungry. Then I would pull the covers off of him and he would finally get up.

We played games together and I would run around the street on Charlie's scooter. He would tell me that all of his friends were watching me.

It was fun watching him grow up to be the young man he is—his Bar Mitzvah, his school, being a teacher's assistant in school, doing so many wonderful things. He was always helpful and smart. We know he will reach his goals because he is very focused and able to study and not be distracted by anything else.

David

My father, Kople, said to Berry one time, "You better watch out because if you don't watch out, I'm going to come back and live with you." Kople had a saying, "Don't marry a woman who has thin lips and boney shoulders." One time Charlie went to a play and said he did not like the lead actress "because she had thin lips and boney shoulders." We all nearly fell on the floor.

When I looked at Charlie for the first time, Charlie looked at me, as if he were saying, "You better watch out, because I know you." The back of his neck looks exactly like my father's and he has a way of concentrating with his eyes closing half-way, as if he can tell if you're being truthful or not.

Charlie always had the patience of a saint. When Legos were popular, he could sit and create a city out of them. We love him very much. Charlie is a very smart young man and we look forward to great accomplishments from him. I think that he's going to surprise all of us.

Top row (left to right): Jerry, Michael, Sara, Joe, Elisa Rose, Joshua. Middle row: Jerry Kaufman, Bryna, Yetta, David, Berry, Teri. Bottom: Alex, Lindsay, Charlie, Emily, David Z.

The wedding. Left to right: Ben and Bertha Solnit, David, Helen and Kople.

Chapter Six

Mishpokhe, Naches and Parnose
FAMILY, JOY AND EARNINGS

David

We were living in Long Beach at 4101 Linden Avenue, the corner of Carson and Linden. We were reading the paper in bed at 8:30 or 9:30 at night and an ad said that there was a house for sale at 354 East Carson Boulevard—that it used to be a senior citizen's home. We called the agent up and I said, "Can you come and show it to us?" He said, "But it's dark. There's no light in there." I said, "Why don't you come and show it to us with a flashlight?" He said, "Are you kidding?" But he met us there and said the owners wanted $32,500 or $33,000. I said, "Offer him $28,000." The place was neglected and dirty.

We went back and forth on the price and finally I said "I'll give you a $500 check right now, but $29,500 is my limit." He took the check and wrote up the deal and by Sunday afternoon it was ours. Then we applied through the State of California and got a license for six people.

But to fix the place, we couldn't get people to clean it up so we had to clean it ourselves. We called cleaning companies and when they saw it, they all said no.

Yetta

I put on a one-piece overall and a big pair of dark glasses and a hat. I took Jerry with me, he was two at the time, and we cleaned the place.

David

At the beginning, Yetta used to cook and taught the housekeepers so the people got good food and good care. Then my wife went to doctors—what I call PDC, Personal Direct Contact, and introduced herself and told them that we owned Bixby Knolls Manor, and would they do us a favor and come by around lunchtime to see what we were feeding the residents. We knew we would make a good impression. Some came, and one of the doctors told a lawyer about us and he put his mother in our manor. We filled it within a couple of months, and we sent the kids to camp so we were able to work with that and the Temple. I helped Yetta when I wasn't busy at the Temple. That was our first business venture.

Then we bought 419–420 East Carson Boulevard. We went around asking our neighbors if they would object to our turning it into a nursing home. There were churches there and a doctor's office across the street, so they couldn't really object. By that time, we had twelve people.

After awhile, our friend, Mr. Samuel Lackman, a well-known attorney in Long Beach, blessed memory, told us about 420 Grand Avenue, by the ocean, which we called Belmont Heights Manor. It used to be a small convalescent hospital, but the people wrecked it and it had been empty for two to three years. It was a disaster. You could see the sky. It was up for court sale the next day.

Yetta

David dressed up, so the court mistook him for an attorney. He told them he was the bidder on the property. They originally wanted around $400,000 and there were three mortgages. All of them died. $175,000 was still owed on it, and it needed over $100,000 to open the doors. The court said, "There's nobody else here, young man. What do you bid?" David said, "$60,000." And they said, "Sold."

I told David I could fix it up. He thought it couldn't be done, but I told him I could do it. We were able to move in with $15,000; the roof was fixed, the kitchen had new tiles. The beds were all good, solid metal, but they were rusty and the mattresses were horrible. I called a company that painted appliances and they spray painted everything a light cream color; everything looked brand new. The nightstands and the beds and the mattress coils they spray painted with aluminum—like silver. I sent out the mattresses to be sanitized like brand new. I paid the interior painters $25 a day and all the food they could eat.

David

The toilets were full of feathers and feces and drugs, and no cleaning company would touch the place. So Yetta put on rubber gloves and goggles and poured lye in the toilets.

Yetta

There were 14 very expensive, hospital commodes that would cost $500 each in those days. They were made of beautiful porcelain. First we took out all the stuff that was in the toilets and then poured in the lye. It was like seeing a diamond. We were never afraid of a little hard work to make the business successful.

In the dining room I put beautiful canary-yellow shades and lamps, with round tables and chairs that were also cream colored. I made drapes and bought dishes, linens and towels. I filled the place in two to three months. Now I had three places to take care of, plus my own home.

I used to have a lot of staff that didn't speak English and when they were sober, they worked beautifully. When they were drunk, they were nobody.

We weren't fancy, but we were very clean. We gave good service, good food and it was like a family. We had the Belmont Heights business for about ten years, but altogether, we were in the business for about 26 years. The woman who bought it from us was an African-American woman by the name of Mrs. White. She was a lovely lady.

Mr. Herman Gunther was one of our guests. He was a wonderful man and a plumber and a musician in Germany. He told us he was Irish. He was a prince of a man and he stayed with us over two years in our house. The children loved him and he loved the children. He said, "Mrs. Kane, your children are angels."

I would get up at six in the morning and by seven o'clock, everything was done. Mr. Gunther would eat breakfast at seven-thirty and I would feed my husband. David would go to Temple and the children would go to school. I went on a bicycle from the Elm Avenue house to the Carson nursing home. I would take Jerry on the back with me because we had only one car.

The people working for me didn't speak English, and if I asked them to make a piece of toast, they would put it in their hand and bring it to me like that. No plate. Most of them didn't know how to read and write. They were nice people, with good hearts, and they worked hard.

I worked seven days a week—every single day, every holiday. But I always went to the Temple with the children every Friday night and every Shabbat.

Rabbi Kane with Confirmation candidates at Temple Beth Shalom, 1962. Andrea Fox front row, second left, transcribed the interviews for this memoir, 49 years later.

I had another lady by the name of Esther Sitker. Esther was a lovely lady, but she had one problem. She would walk up and down the corridor constantly. She only stopped when she slept or ate. At times, when her medicine didn't kick in, she had a mean streak. A lot of people when they have dementia, think everyone is stealing from them. She would tell me I stole her stockings. I would tell her that I didn't like the color and they wouldn't fit me anyway.

One day Esther slapped her roommate. I sat them both down, and I always did this with another person in the room so there would be no

question about what happened. I said, "Esther, why did you slap her?" Esther said the other lady stole her stockings and wouldn't give them back. I slapped her as hard as I could on her foot and I asked if she liked being slapped. I asked her if she thought the lady liked it when she did it to her. She started to cry, apologized and kissed my hand. She never did it again.

David and Yetta
with cousin, Minnie
Kaplan.

David's 80th birthday party. Left to right: Morris, Sara, Yetta and (front) Herman.

The Love Boat Rabbi and Rabbizin.

$\mathcal{T}$HE LOVE BOAT RABBI

$\mathcal{D}$avid

After I retired from Temple Beth Shalom, I became the Love Boat Rabbi with various cruise lines: Cunard, Princess Lines and Holland America. For $75 a day, we got room and board on the ship. We went on over 40 cruises. We went to China, Japan, Germany, Russia and we even went to Egypt and Israel. We went to Australia, New Zealand, Greece, Turkey, Malaysia and the South Pacific. All through Europe and the Scandinavian countries. Sorrento and Italy.

We couldn't have afforded to do this paying for it ourselves. We only had to pay for getting to the ship and returning home, and gratuities. I gave services on Friday night and Saturday morning and on holidays. Sometimes I would give a lecture. There were a lot of things to do on the ship; movies, art shows, entertainment, lectures and excursions. We met people from all over the world who spoke every language under the sun. Our linguistic abilities gave us good standing.

We collected a lot of things. Our dining-room set and my office furniture, we bought in Sorrento, Italy. We sent it home in a big container. We got a silver egg to commemorate Passover in Istanbul. It says: Let My People Go. We got one of our Torahs, believe it or not, in Ketchikan, Alaska; a Judaica store like you would see on Rodeo Drive. It is a replica of the Torah that was built in Mannheim, Germany—all silver and gold. We bought two brass candelabra in Rome, and some yardage goods from St. Kitts, the French side, in St. Croix. We were in Berlin when the wall was knocked down. We were in Hungary and in Prague and Budapest. We went to Vienna, Costa Rica and Pompeii.

Yetta

We went to where Hitler, Stalin and Churchill signed the treaty in Germany, and where the Nuremberg Trials took place. Going through the Panama Canal was unbelievable —we went through it three times. In Malaysia, I touched the Golden Buddha—500 pounds of solid gold. The monks had him covered up with tar—like a tepee—they were afraid invaders would come and steal him or chop off pieces. So they were smart and hid him. Many years later some monks decided they wanted to move the Buddha to a different place, so they picked him up on a huge, huge crane and the cable broke and it fell down. They saw something shining in the cracks and little by little, they chiseled away at it, and found a solid gold Buddha. They loved the Buddha and built a house for him—it's a shrine. You're not allowed to go inside and there's chains all around the outside. But I stepped over the chain and rubbed his stomach.

When we were in Israel at the Beth Ehlyon court house, it was just finished. It's something unbelievable to see; the most fascinating court house I have ever seen in the entire world. Everything was done in beautiful mahogany wood; the cabinets, the walls, everything. The courtyard was built like in biblical times, with a little light coming in from the ceiling, going around like a crown where the sun shines in. There was a clock like in olden times that would strike at noon. We took Elisa with us for her Bat Mitzvah.

We were in Rothschild's wine garden in Israel. It was called The Garden of the Roses. We also visited the Hadassah Hospital where they have the windows created by the great artist Marc Chagall. It's a big, round room with benches so you can sit and admire everything. I understand they took the windows out and stored them for safekeeping.

Front and back views of a silver egg acquired in Istanbul. It depicts the Passover Seder, and Pharaoh with Jewish slaves. The Hebrew engraving is a blessing said over Matzah.

Sterling silver miniature Torah scroll with gold accents, open.

Chapter Seven

God, Gezunt and a little philosophy

David on positive thinking

Because we survived, all of life has meaning, whether it's a terrible happening or whether it's a great joy. I'll illustrate what I mean with a joke. A fellow breaks his leg and he's all bandaged up. He's laughing like crazy and someone says to him, "Why are you laughing? You broke a leg. Do you think that's funny?" The man answers, "You're crazy. Do you realize I could have broken both legs?"

On gratitude

Gratitude is a way to get joy in your heart. If somebody does something good for me, I enjoy feeling grateful and thankful, to acknowledge it. You cannot mimic gratitude, you cannot pretend gratitude—it's a way of life. Two words—thank you—have a tremendous punch in life. A tremendous influence. Like my wife says—a smile doesn't cost anything, but you can make someone else's day rich with it.

Yetta on gratitude

To be a happy, healthy person, I'm grateful for everything—for each moment I breathe, for each moment I'm above ground, for each moment I'm alive, for the friends we have, for the knowledge God blessed us with, for being able to function like "normal human beings." If you can provide for yourself physically, mentally and financially, it's important to be grateful. Financial isn't the most important part, but you cannot get along without it.

David on atheism

There is a saying in Hebrew that you cannot be a pious person just by mouthing it, you have to be active in it. You cannot be an ignoramus or a non-believer unless you were a believer first. I like to tell the joke about the atheist who meets his friend on the street and the friend says, "How is your atheism going? He replies, "I gave it up." The friend says, "What happened?" He replies, "They don't have enough holidays."

David on choosing a marriage partner

When you get married, if you're lucky enough to get the right partner in life, and you're honest, you can make your life beautiful or you can make your life miserable. It's what you choose. In the Bible, it says, *I've given you, man, a choice this day.* You can take it for a blessing or you can take it for a curse. It depends on where you want to go. If a man has a good wife, he has a better, longer life. And that has been proven by scientists.

David reflects on the Holocaust

The concentration camps that I went through and the horrors I went through, I pray that no person in this world will ever go through. But I am very, very grateful that I have reached my age and I can look back and be thankful to God that I have survived. Each day that God gives me, I learn something new and for each year that I get older, I am forever grateful.

There was a time when my life could be taken from me at any moment. At one time I wanted to run into the electric wires in the concentration camp and kill myself. To come to this point where my psyche is strong now, is the greatest thing in the world. I can never believe that I ever wanted to do that. That's how low my mental state was. My morals were always very high but I never believed that I would grow up to get a life out of the camp. I never thought I would lead a normal life or fall in love and get married and have children and grandchildren. Now, thanks to God, I have become a great grandfather. I mean, this is a miraculous happening.

Back then we were depressed. We were in hell, like my wife says. We had no food, no clothing, no sanitation. It was the lowest degree of human existence. You were worse than a dog in a concentration camp. The dog was respected more than we were. The only reason I was there was because I was born Jewish. I didn't steal, I did not murder anyone, I did not do anything wrong, and yet I was incarcerated and people like me were burned in crematoriums, alive. For what? Because of our faith.

P'samim (a spice box) for Havdalah, ushering out the Sabbath.

On hate

I transcend it in a very simple way. I have no feeling of injustice toward the German people who were born after 1945 and 1946, or the German people whose children were born yesterday or are going to be born tomorrow. My feeling of injustice is reserved for their fathers and grandfathers, and Hitler. He was a demented, syphilitic corporal, who was a painter, and became the head of the German nation. It's almost unbelievable because the German world, before the war, was a very intelligent, educated country. Yet, they followed the dictates and wishes of this evil murderer. He wanted to control the whole world. He wanted to conquer the whole world. If it wasn't for certain nations, the Russians or the United States and England, and those that fought against him, he would've killed the world. I said to myself, "Am I going to hate everybody because of this man? Am I going to hate everybody because of the Gestapo? Am I going to hate a man who was born in 1946 or 1947 because his grandfather was a Gestapo?" My answer is, "No."

Do you know how many times I wake up and that sound of my grandfather, Menachem Mendel Koplowicz, as he is being shot, is in my head? I don't forgive the SS and Germany for having created the wound in my heart and head. I cannot forget. I can forgive and not blame future generations and the present generation because they had nothing to do with it. That's how I transcend it.

Yetta and the Mikvah

For many years, I was known as the "Mikvah Lady." When people needed a mikvah, the ritual bath, if it was warm, I took them to the ocean. They would wear a large dress, say the prayer, and go under. Later we used our swimming pool and then we started going to the University of Judaism. I liked the ocean. When we went to the ocean we didn't have to pay anything.

David and the Reverts

I got my ordination at 27 years old in 1957. I started reverting people in 1955, with the Rabbi Moshe Magal, who was the head of the Rabbinical Court. I call converts "reverts," because at one time the whole world was Jewish. There's a sentence that we pray called Gayray Tzedek for the righteous proselyte. They are in the beginning of our daily prayers. We reverted more than one hundred people during our years in Los Angeles.

On the Jewish people

Today we have Orthodox Jews (Lubavitch), Conservative Jews, Reconstruction Jews, we have Reform Judaism. To me, I'm sure Yetta feels the same way… a Jew is a Jew is a Jew. I have no labels—I don't care if he or she is Orthodox, Reform, Conservative, whatever. It's a Jewish person. In order to be happy, you have to be happy with whatever you are.

David on Israel

The Torah says to get yourself a teacher. Make a friend and get yourself a teacher. Why get a teacher? So you can learn how to provide for yourself.

The Arabs have so much oil and so much land. Israel is a miniscule part of that area. Israel doesn't have that much land, but look what they have done with it. In 1948, sixty-two years ago, Israel was created. Look what they've accomplished in the world with a little piece of land. Everybody toiled, everybody worked, and everybody used their brains. The Jewish people are called The People of the Book (Am HaSafer). They have studied, created and developed—whether science or land, or whatever, they just didn't sit around. They had to produce in order to survive, so they produced things that they sold to the world.

America today

Part of the problem we have in America today is that we are a service country. We are not a producing country. We're not manufacturing. We outsource to China, India, to wherever. You call up some manufacturer about a product and somebody in India or China answers the phone. That's no good.

An education is the basic ingredient of advancement. If you don't teach a child to be able to count, to be able to know where things come from or how they develop, then how do you expect to grow? We're falling behind in America. There's no free breakfast. You have to contribute your ability, your knowledge and your willingness, to do that. Entitlement is a great part of life, but some people take advantage of entitlement. They think that everything is coming to them. In California, we have been under the impression that there is a free breakfast. That's why now in 2011, we're billions of dollars in debt.

The Rabbi's hands, holding a wooden Haftora given in 1976 at his official Bar Mitzvah at Temple Beth Shalom, Long Beach. This is just one of the many generous gifts from the congregation.

What we learned from our parents

Yetta

I was blessed. I came from a home where there was love and compassion and belief in God. Even when we went hungry, we prayed, and my mother, Edla, told us that tomorrow would be a better day. We had no pen and no paper, but we still had to practice a little reading and writing. During the war, Edla and Zelik couldn't give us material things, shelter or food, but they could give us love and transmit the knowledge they had in their minds and souls. My father could get up and do Haftorah, by heart, in Hebrew.

David

My mother-in-law, Edla, was like a mother to me. My father-in-law, Zelik, was a very wise businessman—very hardworking, so we had very good examples. We remember Kople and Brajndla, and their efforts and sacrifice every day. We have tried to live by the wisdom they taught us, and we've tried to pass it on to our children, grandchildren and great grandchildren. What our parents and grandparents taught lives in us, and will live forever in the generations that come after us, God willing.

The End

Yetta and David
celebrate Elisa
and Joshua's
wedding, 2005.

L'Dor Vador

What our parents and grandparents taught
lives in us, and will live forever
in the generations that come after us,
God willing.